cakes & bakes

from my mother's kitchen

RYLAND
PETERS
& SMALL
LONDON NEW YORK

cakes & bakes
from my mother's kitchen

contributing editor Linda Collister

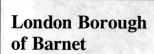

London Borough of Barnet	
Askews	Jan-2010
641.8653	£16.99

Senior Designer Sonya Nathoo
Commissioning Editor Julia Charles
Picture Researcher Emily Westlake
Production Controller Hazel Kirkman
Art Director Leslie Harrington
Publishing Director Alison Starling
Indexer Hilary Bird

First published in the UK in 2010
by Ryland Peters & Small
20–21 Jockey's Fields
London WC1R 4BW
www.rylandpeters.com

10 9 8 7 6 5 4 3 2 1

Text © Linda Collister, Susannah Blake,
Maxine Clark, Ross Dobson, Brian Glover,
Fran Warde, Liz Franklin, Laura Washburn 2010
Design and photographs
© Ryland Peters & Small 2010

Printed in China

ISBN: 978 1 84597 949 2

A CIP record for this book is available from the
British Library.

Notes
• All spoon measurements are level, unless
otherwise specified.
• All eggs are medium, unless otherwise specified.
It is generally recommended that free-range eggs be
used. Uncooked or partially cooked eggs should not
be served to the very young, the very old, those with
compromised immune systems, or to pregnant
women.
• Ovens should be preheated to the specified
temperature. Recipes in this book were tested using
a regular oven. If using a fan-assisted oven, follow
the manufacturer's instructions for adjusting
temperatures.
• When a recipe calls for the zest of lemons or limes,
buy unwaxed fruit and wash well before using. If you
can only find treated fruit, scrub well in warm soapy
water and rinse before using.

contents

A passion for baking

For me, baking combines many pleasures; creative pride in the making, social satisfaction in the sharing and sensual delight in the eating. But it also brings to mind many fond memories not only of special celebrations and family meals, but also of time spent enjoyably in the kitchen as a child. Nothing beats home-made: a proper cake that tastes of real butter and fresh eggs; pastry that truly melts in the mouth; an honest loaf of bread with a complex flavour, a good texture and a chewy crust; biscuits scented with real vanilla; intensely chocolatey brownies.

The food we adored as children, made with love by parents and grandparents, stays with us for life. Although my own mother was a fantastic hostess who loved food, she wasn't a great cook, but I'm lucky enough to remember cooking with my grandmother before I started school. She was born in the 19th century and time spent with her in the warm kitchen, with its bright curtains and delicious smell of cakes baking in the enamel gas stove, was the ultimate treat. Turning scraps of pastry dough into jam tarts and cheese straws was a bigger adventure than a trip to the swings. We began with bag of flour, a carton of eggs, a scoop of sugar and a brick of butter and we ended up with a cake: magic! I was free to explore the pantry, to create my own 'recipes', to half-secretly lick out the bowl. Even washing up with a mountain of bubbles in a butler's sink as deep as a bathtub was a delight. Now I feel as if I have always baked.

From my grandmother, a true Women's Institute baker, I learnt how to make the best cookies and the lightest sponge cakes. Her house and habits were from an age that has completely disappeared. She had a cool, dark pantry, in which she always kept a home-cooked ham, a truckle of Cheddar, and a Dundee cake, along with the jams, marmalades and pickles necessary for unexpected guests and emergencies. She had a far more limited range of ingredients than we do now and these were mostly locally produced, had to be fresh and in season. But she never scrimped on quality – only unsalted butter, fresh thick cream, the best flour and proper chocolate would do.

My grandmother's style of baking required a lot of preparation. Flour had to be sifted twice, while dried fruit had to be picked over, washed carefully and dried overnight on a tea towel. The heavy sugar syrup had to be rinsed off the candied peel and cherries before chopping. Hunks of suet bought from the butcher were grated and tossed in flour before use in Christmas puddings or a jam roly-poly. She had high standards and strong views. She would not tolerate lumps in batter, dough or icing.

Opening the oven door during baking was almost sinful. But she also believed that absolutely anyone could cook.

Good cooks are always happy to share recipes and pass on tips and techniques. My mother-in-law from Maine has taught me how to bake in the finest American tradition. Now in her mid-eighties, she still loves to revive old favourites and to experiment with new recipes. With a well-travelled family of a food-loving husband, five children and eight grandchildren to indulge, she still has plenty of opportunities to bake. We had barely been introduced when she mailed me the first of many packages. 'You'll be needing these for Thanksgiving' read the covering note on the typewritten sheets. I had no idea I was expected to cook this peculiarly American meal, let alone what to make, so her recipe collection of old-fashioned New England pies and tarts was indeed welcome. I still bring it out each November. I must admit I was thrilled the first time she asked me for a special recipe for the Holidays! Our experience is not unusual. Most families develop and establish their own traditions over many years, if not generations. And like so many these days, ours is a family of diverse backgrounds, nationalities and tastes, so each year we experiment. On the table, beside every eagerly anticipated annual treat, sits an innovation. This year's innovation, of course, may become next year's tradition.

Nowadays most of us only bake when we want to, not when we have to. So it seems strange that for many of the older generation it was an everyday task. Now we no longer need to bake in order to put a loaf on the table for breakfast, baking has become an enjoyable hobby for many cooks keen to learn new skills. Baking is still the gesture of love, friendship and giving it always was, but now we bake for pleasure, for the fun of watching a colleague open a box of cupcakes piped with Happy Birthday; sharing flapjacks and a flask of coffee on a day out; savouring a warm slice of cake in front of the fire on a wet weekend. Baking expresses love, gratitude and comradeship, and the time and thought involved is always appreciated. My young daughter has never forgotten the time she and a couple of friends baked trays of chocolate muffins to celebrate the birthday of their very popular form teacher. He was so taken aback that he disappeared, speechless for once, into the staff room with the muffins. To the girls' amazement (and horror), he shared them with his cheering colleagues rather than his eager pupils. I was surprised at his surprise; children love baking, showing off the results – then scoffing the lot.

Nothing beats home-made for taste but also for freshness and quality. Shop-bought cakes and desserts often contain many ingredients you've never heard of, as well as unhealthy fats and the preservatives needed to give them a longer shelf-life. With food you bake yourself, you can pick the ingredients you want to eat – unsalted butter rather than vegetable fat, free-range eggs, Fair Trade or Organic sugar, fruit and chocolate. You can ensure that nothing has traces of nuts or contains animal products. You are in control! Home baking also saves money. A whole batch of fudgy chocolate-heavy brownies costs about the same as one square in a fashionable coffee shop, and nothing in the supermarket can compare with home-made biscuits.

Over the years I've discovered what I really need to bake well. It's good to have an oven thermometer to check the temperature – crucial for baking delicate biscuits and pastries. In the past I've had to wire one oven door shut and wedge open another using a wooden spoon to maintain the right temperature when the thermostat was inaccurate. I also rely on an accurate timer. A few minutes here or there will not affect a casserole, but can prove fatal for a cake. Accurate measures are also vital to success, so a set of good-quality weighing scales is a necessity, along with a measuring jug and spoons. Wooden spoons, plastic scrapers, a couple of mixing bowls and a sieve will do for most simple recipes, but it's worth investing in an electric hand whisk for sponge cakes and meringues. A large free-standing mixer is not cheap, but it will take the hard work out of kneading bread dough, making heavy cake mixtures, and whisking egg whites. A food processor is excellent for pastry, scones, certain biscuits and cookies, fillings for cheesecakes and chopping nuts and chocolate.

It is worth spending a bit on good quality bakeware. Tins and trays should be the right size to fit your oven. They should be made of a good heavy duty material to prevent scorching and the tray buckling in a hot oven. They will also be less likely to rust or become dented with heavy use. I've been using my baking trays, bread and cake tins day in and day out for over 20 years and they are still in good heart. A large wire cooling rack plus a wide spatula for lifting biscuits and scones will also be handy. And you will need a heavy oven glove for handling hot tins and trays; tea towels are no substitute, and damp ones can be dangerous. You will need to store your bakes in good sturdy airtight containers or tins. Bread is always best stored in a cool, dark spot in a box designed for the purpose.

Before you begin, it's worth re-reading the recipe to check you have everything you need to hand. Remove the butter and eggs from the fridge soon enough to let them come to room temperature if necessary. Preheat the oven and prepare the baking tins. Then put on some music and relax – it's just food, and however it turns out it will always taste wonderful and be truly appreciated.

Linda Collister

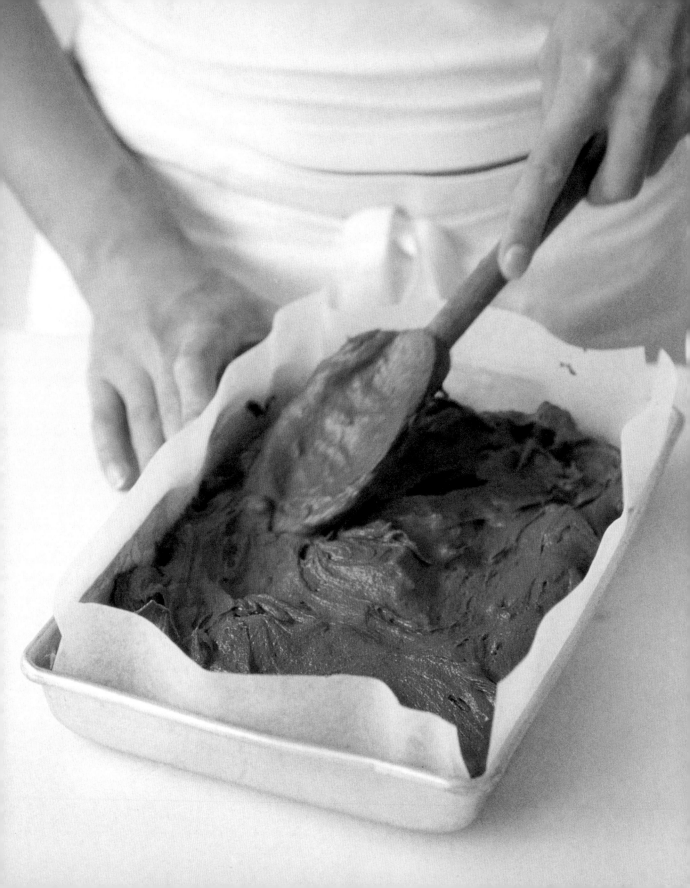

cookies, brownies & bars

double chocolate chip cookies

These are large, flat cookies, perfect for sandwiching together with ice cream. To make smaller ones for eating with a glass of cold milk or a milkshake, use smaller spoonfuls and don't spread the mixture out. Although real chocolate chopped into pieces tastes better, it won't hold its shape as nicely as ready-made chocolate chips, but it is up to you which you choose.

75 g unsalted butter, softened

75 g golden caster sugar

75 g light soft brown sugar

1 large egg, beaten

½ teaspoon vanilla extract

150 g self-raising flour

25 g cocoa powder

¼ teaspoon salt

100 g dark and white (or milk) chocolate chips or chopped dark chocolate

several baking trays, greased

makes about 12 large cookies

Preheat the oven to 180°C (350°F) Gas 4.

Using an electric mixer, cream the butter and sugars together in a large bowl until pale and fluffy. Beat in the egg and vanilla extract.

Sift the flour with the cocoa and salt in a small bowl. Fold into the egg mixture with the chocolate chips.

Place 4 heaped tablespoons of the mixture on the prepared baking tray, spacing them well apart. Press down and spread out to about 5 mm thick with the back of a wet spoon or with dampened fingers (you may like to scatter some more chocolate chips over the top).

Bake in the preheated oven for 10–12 minutes. Leave to cool on the baking tray for a few minutes, then transfer to a wire rack to cool completely. Repeat with the remaining mixture. When cool, store in an airtight container and eat within 5 days or freeze for up to 1 month.

Baking Tip: If baked cookies are stuck to the baking tray, return the tray to the oven briefly – the cookies should then lift off easily.

pumpkin seed cookies

Seeds are not only tasty but good for you. A great way to enjoy them is to add them to cookies, and these ones are really quick and easy to make and guaranteed to become a family cookie jar favourite.

200 g self-raising flour

125 g butter, cut into cubes

125 g light muscovado sugar

1 egg, beaten

75 g pumpkin seeds

several baking trays, greased

makes about 20 cookies

Preheat the oven to 180°C (350°F) Gas 4.

Put the flour, butter and sugar in a bowl and mix with a fork until the mixture resembles breadcrumbs. Add the egg and seeds, mix again and form into a ball.

Lightly flour a work surface and use your hands to roll the dough into a sausage shape about 20 cm long. Cut into about 20 slices and place on the prepared baking trays. Bake in the preheated oven for about 12–15 minutes.

Leave to cool for a few minutes on the baking trays, then transfer to a wire rack to cool completely. When cool, store in an airtight container and eat within 5 days or freeze for up to 1 month.

Baking Tip: If you run out of self-raising flour, sift together 4 level teaspoons of baking powder with every 250 g plain flour. This will not create quite such a high lift as self-raising flour when baking cakes but makes a good substitute for cookies.

classic oat cookies

These cookies are always popular, whether flavoured with dried fruit or spices or left plain. It's important to use old-fashioned porridge oats or rolled oats rather than 'instant' oats.

115 g unsalted butter, very soft

140 g light muscovado sugar

1 large egg, beaten

1 tablespoon whole milk

½ teaspoon vanilla extract

100 g self-raising flour

75 g dried fruit, such as raisins, sultanas, cherries, cranberries or blueberries

150 g porridge oats

several baking trays, greased

makes about 24 cookies

Preheat the oven to 180°C (350°F) Gas 4.

Put the butter, sugar, egg, milk and vanilla extract in a bowl and beat well using an electric mixer or whisk, or a wooden spoon. Add the flour, dried fruit and oats and mix well with a wooden spoon. Put heaped teaspoons of cookie dough onto the prepared baking trays, spacing them well apart.

Bake in the preheated oven for 12–15 minutes until lightly browned around the edges.

Leave to cool on the baking trays for a few minutes, then transfer to a wire rack to cool completely. When cool, store in an airtight container and eat within 5 days or freeze for up to 1 month.

Variations: Omit the dried fruit and at the same time as the flour, add either 1 teaspoon ground cinnamon, 1 teaspoon mixed spice and 2 pinches of freshly ground black pepper, or 60 g chocolate chips and 25 g chopped almonds.

chocolate crackle cookies

These dark chocolate cookies have a pretty white 'crazy-paving' top – an effect that is created by rolling the cookies in icing sugar just before baking. The surface then cracks to form the 'paving'.

100 g dark chocolate, broken into pieces

115 g unsalted butter, cut into cubes

175 g light muscovado sugar

1 large egg, beaten

2–3 drops vanilla extract

175 g self-raising flour

½ teaspoon bicarbonate of soda

2 tablespoons icing sugar

several baking trays, greased

makes about 24 cookies

Preheat the oven to 200°C (400°F) Gas 6.

Put the chocolate, butter and sugar in a heatproof bowl and set over a saucepan of gently simmering water. Melt gently, stirring occasionally until smooth.

Remove the bowl from the saucepan and leave to cool for a minute. Stir in the egg, vanilla extract, flour and bicarbonate of soda and mix well. Cover the bowl and chill until the mixture is firm, about 20 minutes.

Put the icing sugar in a shallow dish. Using your hands, roll the dough into walnut-sized balls, then roll in the icing sugar to coat thoroughly. Set the balls on the prepared baking trays, spacing them well apart. Bake in the preheated oven for about 10–12 minutes until just set.

Leave to cool on the baking tray for a few minutes, then transfer to a wire rack to cool completely. Store in an airtight container and eat within 5 days or freeze for up to 1 month.

Baking Tip: Most home-made cookies freeze well. Seal them in freezer bags or pack in rigid, airtight, plastic containers and freeze for up to 1 month. Defrost for several hours at room temperature before eating.

classic choc chip cookies

These simple cookies are always popular and hard to beat! The classic recipe has been adapted here so that it uses less sugar and more nuts. Use plain chocolate broken up into chunks or a bag of chocolate chips, as preferred.

175 g self-raising flour

a pinch of salt

a good pinch of bicarbonate of soda

115 g unsalted butter, very soft

60 g caster sugar

60 g light muscovado sugar

½ teaspoon vanilla extract

1 large egg, lightly beaten

175 g dark chocolate, broken into pieces, or chocolate chips

75 g walnut or pecan pieces

several baking trays, greased

makes about 24 cookies

Preheat the oven to 190°C (375°F) Gas 5.

Put all the ingredients in a large bowl and mix thoroughly with a wooden spoon.

Drop heaped teaspoons of the mixture onto the prepared baking trays, spacing them well apart.

Bake in the preheated oven for 8–10 minutes until lightly coloured and just firm.

Leave to cool on the baking trays for a minute, then transfer to a wire rack to cool completely.

When completely cool, store in an airtight container and eat within 5 days or freeze for up to 1 month.

soured cream and spice brownies

Ginger and chocolate is a delicious taste combination. Here, very good dark chocolate flavoured with pieces of crystallized ginger is used in a dark chocolate mixture. Just a hint of spice, plus deliciously tangy soured cream, makes these grown-up brownies extra special.

200 g dark chocolate

100 g unsalted butter

4 large eggs

200 g caster sugar

100 g plain flour

¼ teaspoon ground cinnamon

½ teaspoon ground ginger

3 tablespoons soured cream

50-g bar dark chocolate with ginger pieces, chopped

a brownie tin, 20.5 x 25.5 cm, greased and base-lined with baking paper

makes 20 brownies

Preheat the oven to 180°C (350°F) Gas 4.

Break up the dark chocolate and put it in a heatproof mixing bowl with the butter. Set the bowl over a pan of simmering water and melt gently, stirring frequently. Remove the bowl from the pan and leave to cool until needed.

Put the eggs and sugar into the bowl of an electric mixer and whisk until very thick and mousse-like. Whisk in the melted chocolate mixture.

Sift the flour and spices into the bowl and stir in. Mix in the soured cream followed by the chopped chocolate with ginger. Transfer to the prepared tin and spread evenly.

Bake in the preheated oven for about 25 minutes, until a skewer inserted halfway between the sides and the centre comes out just clean. Remove the tin from the oven.

Leave to cool completely before removing from the tin and cutting into 20 pieces. Store in an airtight container and eat within 5 days.

old-fashioned brownies

Some brownie enthusiasts believe that only cocoa should be used, not melted dark chocolate, as it gives a deeper, truly intense chocolate flavour which balances the sugar necessary to give a proper fudgy texture. Choose the best quality cocoa powder you can find.

100 g walnut pieces

4 large eggs

300 g caster sugar

140 g unsalted butter, melted

½ teaspoon vanilla extract

140 g plain flour

75 g cocoa powder

a brownie tin, 20.5 x 25.5 cm, greased and base-lined with baking paper

makes 16 brownies

Preheat the oven to 170°C (325°F) Gas 3.

Put the walnut pieces in an ovenproof dish and lightly toast in the preheated oven for about 10 minutes. Remove from the oven and leave to cool. Don't turn off the oven.

Break the eggs into a mixing bowl. Use a hand-held electric mixer to whisk until frothy, then whisk in the sugar. Whisk for a minute then, still whisking constantly, add the melted butter in a steady stream. Whisk for a minute, then whisk in the vanilla.

Sift the flour and cocoa into the bowl and stir in with a wooden spoon. When thoroughly combined, stir in the nuts. Transfer the mixture to the prepared tin and spread evenly.

Bake in the preheated oven for about 25 minutes until a skewer inserted halfway between the sides and the centre comes out just clean. Remove the tin from the oven.

Leave to cool completely before removing from the tin and cutting into 16 pieces. Store in an airtight container and eat within 5 days.

cranberry and dark chocolate brownies

The sharpness of dried cranberries balances the sweetness of this dark chocolate brownie mixture, and the tangy grated orange zest lifts the richness. The flavourings make this a lovely brownie for the festive season.

200 g dark chocolate

200 g unsalted butter, cut into cubes

3 large eggs

175 g caster sugar

finely grated zest of 1 orange

200 g plain flour

100 g dried cranberries

a brownie tin, 20.5 x 25.5 cm, greased and base-lined with baking paper

makes 20 brownies

Preheat the oven to 180°C (350°F) Gas 4.

Break up the chocolate and put it in a heatproof mixing bowl with the butter. Set the bowl over a saucepan of simmering water and melt gently, stirring frequently. Remove the bowl from the pan and leave to cool until needed.

Whisk the eggs in a separate bowl until frothy using an electric mixer or whisk. Add the sugar and orange zest and whisk until the mixture becomes very thick and mousse-like. Whisk in the melted chocolate mixture.

Sift the flour into the mixture and stir in. When everything is thoroughly combined, stir in the dried cranberries. Transfer the mixture to the prepared tin and spread evenly.

Bake in the preheated oven for about 25 minutes, until a skewer inserted halfway between the sides and the centre comes out just clean. Remove the tin from the oven.

Leave to cool completely before removing from the tin and cutting into 20 pieces. Store in an airtight container and eat within 5 days.

Baking Tip: When batch-baking cookies, brownies or bars, once you remove each tray from the oven, let the oven return to the correct cooking temperature before putting in the next batch.

coconut blondies

Slightly sticky and very chewy, these delicious 'blondies' are heavy with coconut as well as dark and white chocolate. You will need to use the unsweetened type of desiccated coconut.

175 g desiccated coconut

175 g unsalted butter

300 g light muscovado sugar

2 large eggs, lightly beaten

1 teaspoon vanilla extract

200 g plain flour

1 teaspoon baking powder

50 g white chocolate, chopped, or white chocolate chips

50 g dark chocolate, chopped, or dark chocolate chips

a brownie tin, 20.5 x 25.5 cm, greased and base-lined with baking paper

makes 20 blondies

Preheat the oven to 180°C (350°F) Gas 4.

Put the coconut in a heatproof baking dish and toast in the preheated oven for about 5 minutes, stirring frequently, until a light golden brown. Remove from the oven and leave to cool. Don't turn off the oven.

Melt the butter in a saucepan set over low heat. Remove the pan from the heat and stir in the sugar with a wooden spoon.

Gradually beat in the eggs, then the vanilla extract. Sift the flour and baking powder into the mixture and stir in. Finally, work in the coconut and both the white and dark chopped chocolate or chocolate chips.

When everything is thoroughly combined, transfer the mixture to the prepared tin and spread evenly.

Bake in the preheated oven for about 20–25 minutes, until golden brown and a skewer inserted halfway between the sides and the centre comes out just clean.

Leave to cool completely before removing from the tin and cutting into 20 pieces. Store in an airtight container and eat within 5 days.

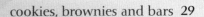

sticky coffee bars

These wonderfully moist bars studded with chocolate chips, hazelnuts and sticky fudge fall somewhere between a brownie and a cookie. They're divine served slightly warm, but they're pretty sensational served cold as well.

150 g unsalted butter, at room temperature

100 g caster sugar

100 g light soft brown sugar

1 tablespoon instant coffee dissolved in 1 tablespoon just-boiled water

1 large egg

225 g self-raising flour

60 g dark chocolate, chopped, or dark chocolate chips

70 g whole blanched hazelnuts, roughly chopped

70 g vanilla fudge, chopped

a cake tin, 20-cm square, greased and lined with baking paper

makes 12 bars

Preheat the oven to 190°C (375°F) Gas 5.

Beat the butter and caster and brown sugars together in a bowl until smooth and creamy. Beat in the coffee, followed by the egg. Sift over the flour and fold in, then fold in the chocolate chips, hazelnuts and fudge.

Spoon the mixture into the prepared cake tin, spread evenly, and bake in the preheated oven for about 25 minutes until golden and risen.

Leave to cool in the tin for about 5 minutes before cutting into 12 bars. Leave to cool for a little longer in the tin before carefully peeling off the lining paper.

Store in an airtight container and eat within 3 days.

lemon squares

Lemon squares are ever-popular and a staple of many a bake sale and coffee morning. This is a rich version that uses thick cream rather than flour in the filling – it's just as easy to make but a lovely luxurious treat for any special occasion. Note that the squares will need to be chilled overnight.

biscuit base:

150 g plain flour

4 tablespoons icing sugar

finely grated zest of ½ a lemon

115 g unsalted butter, chilled and cut into cubes

lemon topping:

3 large eggs, at room temperature

175 g icing sugar, sifted, plus extra to dust

finely grated zest of 2 lemons

freshly squeezed juice of 4 lemons

125 ml double cream

a cake tin, 20.5 cm square, lined with foil

makes 12 squares

Preheat the oven to 180°C (350°F) Gas 4.

To make the base, put the flour, icing sugar and lemon zest into the bowl of a food processor and process for a few seconds until combined. Add the butter and process to make fine crumbs.

Tip into the prepared cake tin and press onto the base with your fingers to make an even layer. Bake in the preheated oven for about 25 minutes until firm and pale golden. Remove from the oven and leave to cool while you make the topping.

To make the topping, crack the eggs into a large jug and beat with a small whisk until broken up. Add the sifted icing sugar and whisk until thoroughly combined. Add the lemon zest and juice and mix thoroughly, then work in the cream.

Return the tin to the oven and slightly pull out the shelf just enough so you can pour the filling into the tin. Gently push the oven shelf back into place, then close the door and reduce the temperature to 170°C (325°F) Gas 3. Bake for about 25 minutes, until just firm.

Put the tin on a wire rack and leave to cool completely, then cover lightly and chill overnight. Use the foil to lift the whole square out of the tin, then cut into 12 pieces and dust with icing sugar. Store in an airtight container in the refrigerator and eat within 3 days.

raspberry and almond slices

These slices packed with fresh juicy raspberries actually taste better the day after they are made, which makes them ideal for preparing ahead of time ready to pack and take on a picnic or into the office.

150 g fresh raspberries, frozen until firm

1 egg

3 tablespoons caster sugar

1 tablespoon plain flour

75 g unsalted butter

almond shortcrust pastry:

50 g ground almonds

200 g plain flour

80 g caster sugar

·125 g unsalted butter, chilled and cut into cubes

icing sugar, to dust

a long rectangular tart tin, 35 x 10 cm, lightly greased

makes 8–10 slices

Preheat the oven to 180°C (350°F) Gas 4.

To make the pastry, put the ground almonds, flour and sugar in a food processor. With the motor running, add a cube of butter at a time until it is all incorporated and the mixture resembles coarse breadcrumbs. Add 2 tablespoons cold water and process until just combined. Be careful not to overprocess the mixture.

Tip the pastry out onto a lightly-floured work surface and knead to form a ball. Roll it out between 2 layers of baking paper until it is about 5 cm longer and 5 cm wider than the tart tin. Carefully lift the pastry into the tin and use your fingers to press it down into the base and sides, letting it overhang. Prick the base all over with a fork and bake in the preheated oven for 20 minutes until lightly golden. Carefully break off the overhanging pastry. Don't turn off the oven.

Put the egg, sugar and flour in a bowl and use a balloon whisk to beat until thick and pale. Put the butter in a small saucepan and set over medium heat. Leave to melt until frothy and dark golden with a nutty aroma. Working quickly, pour the melted butter over the egg mixture and beat well. Scatter the frozen raspberries into the tart case. Pour the warm batter over the raspberries. Bake in the still-hot oven for about 45 minutes, until the top resembles a golden meringue.

Leave to cool in the tin for at least 30 minutes before dusting with icing sugar and cutting into slices. Store in an airtight container and eat within 2 days.

flapjack squares

Flapjacks are not only delicious but they are packed with nutritious oats and make a sustaining snack that keeps you going for hours. The drizzle of melted chocolate is an optional treat but highly recommended!

200 g unsalted butter

1 tablespoon golden syrup

200 g light soft brown sugar

250 g rolled oats

100–200 g good-quality dark chocolate, melted (optional)

a baking tin, 20 x 30 cm, greased and base-lined with baking paper

makes 8 squares

Preheat the oven to 150°C (300°F) Gas 2.

Melt the butter in a large saucepan, add the golden syrup and sugar and stir until the sugar has dissolved.

Remove the pan from the heat and stir in the oats. Spoon the mixture into the prepared baking tin and bake in the preheated oven for about 20 minutes, until golden. Cut into squares straightaway and leave to cool.

Drizzle the melted chocolate over the flapjacks in a zigzag pattern and allow to set before removing from the tin. Store in an airtight container and eat within 3 days.

Variation: To make Nutty Jacks, simply replace 50 g of the rolled oats with 50 g chopped mixed nuts.

cupcakes & muffins

passion fruit butterfly cakes

Who doesn't remember these pretty little cakes from their childhood – no children's birthday party was complete without a plate of them on the tea table and they are great fun for little hands to make. This recipe is flavoured with fresh passion fruit and makes a welcome treat for a special occasion.

3 passion fruit

115 g unsalted butter, at room temperature

115 g caster sugar

2 eggs

115 g self-raising flour

1 teaspoon baking powder

passion fruit frosting:

6 passion fruit

150 g mascarpone cheese

4 tablespoons icing sugar, plus extra for dusting

a 12-hole muffin tin, lined with paper cases

makes 12 small cakes

Preheat the oven to 180°C (350°F) Gas 4.

Halve the passion fruit. Scoop the flesh into a sieve set over a bowl. Press with the back of a teaspoon to extract the juice.

Beat the butter and sugar together in a bowl until pale and fluffy, then beat in the eggs, one at a time. Sift the flour and baking powder into the mixture and fold in, then stir in the passion fruit juice.

Spoon the cake mixture into the paper cases. Bake in the preheated oven for about 17 minutes, until risen and golden and a skewer inserted in the centre of a cake comes out clean. Transfer to a wire rack and leave to cool.

To make the frosting, halve the passion fruit and scoop the flesh into a sieve set over a bowl. Press with the back of a teaspoon to extract the juice, then add the mascarpone and sifted icing sugar to the bowl. Mix until smooth and creamy. Cover and chill for about 30 minutes to thicken up.

Slice the top off of each cake, then cut each top in half. Spoon a generous dollop of the frosting onto each cake, then top with the two halves, setting them at an angle to resemble wings. Dust with icing sugar to serve. The cakes will keep in an airtight container in the refrigerator for 2 days.

maple and pecan cupcakes

Maple syrup and pecans are a classic combination, and no better anywhere than in these light, sticky cakes topped with creamy, buttery frosting and caramelized pecans. Look out for the darker, amber maple syrup as it has a more intense flavour that really shines through in the fluffy, buttery sponge.

115 g butter, at room temperature

50 g light soft brown sugar

160 ml maple syrup

2 eggs

115 g self-raising flour

60 g pecans, roughly chopped

caramelized pecans:

60 g caster sugar

12 pecan halves

maple frosting:

50 g unsalted butter, at room temperature

3 tablespoons maple syrup

145 g icing sugar

a 12-hole muffin tin, lined with paper cases

makes 12 cupcakes

Preheat the oven to 180°C (350°F) Gas 4.

Beat the butter and sugar together in a large bowl until creamy, then beat in the maple syrup. Beat in the eggs, one at a time, then sift the flour into the mixture and fold in. Fold in the nuts, then spoon the mixture into the paper cases. Bake in the preheated oven for about 17 minutes, until risen and golden and a skewer inserted in the centre of a cake comes out clean. Transfer to a wire rack to cool.

To make the caramelized pecans, put the caster sugar in a saucepan and add 2 tablespoons water. Heat gently, stirring, until the sugar melts and dissolves. Increase the heat and boil for about 6 minutes until it turns a pale gold colour. Spread the nuts out on a sheet of baking paper and spoon over a little of the caramel to cover each nut individually. Leave to cool.

To make the frosting, beat the butter, maple syrup and sifted icing sugar together in a bowl until pale and fluffy. Spread over the cakes and top each one with a caramelized pecan. The cakes will keep in an airtight container in the refrigerator for 2 days.

Baking Tip: When measuring sticky ingredients such as maple syrup, honey or treacle, lightly spray the measuring jug with vegetable oil first. The sticky ingredient should slip easily out of the jug. For smaller amounts, use a metal measuring spoon that has been dipped in hot water.

gooey chocolate and hazelnut cupcakes

With a gooey chocolate and hazelnut centre, these luscious cupcakes are deliciously moreish. Adding chocolate and hazelnut spread to the frosting gives it a lovely nutty taste to complement the toasted hazelnuts on top.

75 g dark chocolate, chopped

100 g unsalted butter, at room temperature

100 g caster sugar

2 eggs

25 g whole blanched hazelnuts, ground

100 g self-raising flour

100 g chocolate and hazelnut spread, such as Nutella

frosting and decoration:

100 g dark chocolate, chopped

100 ml double cream

2 tablespoons chocolate and hazelnut spread, such as Nutella

about 25 g blanched hazelnuts, toasted and cut into large pieces

a 12-hole muffin tin, lined with paper cases

makes 12 cupcakes

Preheat the oven to 180°C (350°F) Gas 4.

Melt the chocolate in a heatproof bowl set over a saucepan of simmering water or in the microwave, then leave to cool.

Beat the butter and sugar together in a bowl until pale and fluffy, then beat in the eggs, one at a time. Stir in the ground hazelnuts, then sift the flour into the mixture and fold in. Stir in the melted chocolate.

Drop ½ heaped tablespoon of the mixture into each paper case, then flatten and make an indentation in the centre of each dollop of mixture using the back of a teaspoon. Drop a generous dollop of chocolate spread into the centre of each one, then top with the remaining cake mixture. Bake in the preheated oven for about 18 minutes until risen and the top of a cake springs back when gently pressed. Transfer to a wire rack and leave to cool.

To make the frosting, put the chocolate in a heatproof bowl. Heat the cream in a saucepan until almost boiling, then pour over the chocolate and leave to stand for 5 minutes. Stir until smooth and creamy, then stir in the chocolate spread. Leave to cool for about 30 minutes until thick and glossy.

Spread the frosting over the cakes and arrange a few nuts in the centre of each one. The cakes will keep in an airtight container in the refrigerator for 2 days.

gingerbread cupcakes with lemon icing

These soft, sticky cakes are packed with spicy ginger and drizzled with a simple lemon icing. If you want elegant flat-topped cakes, make them in large cupcake cases, but if you prefer domed cakes with icing drizzling down the sides, make them in regular-sized cases.

60 g unsalted butter

50 g light soft brown sugar

2 tablespoons golden syrup

2 tablespoons black treacle

1 teaspoon ground ginger

80 ml whole milk

1 egg, beaten

2 pieces of stem ginger in syrup, drained and chopped

115 g self-raising flour

icing and decoration:

2 tablespoons freshly squeezed lemon juice

200 g icing sugar, sifted

2–3 pieces of stem ginger in syrup, drained and chopped

a 12-hole muffin tin, lined with paper cases

makes 12 cupcakes

Preheat the oven to 170°C (325°F) Gas 3.

Put the butter, sugar, golden syrup, treacle and ground ginger in a saucepan and heat gently until melted. Remove the pan from the heat and stir in the milk, then beat in the egg and stem ginger. Pour the mixture into a large bowl and sift in the flour. Fold in until well combined.

Spoon the mixture into the paper cases and bake in the preheated oven for about 20 minutes until risen and a skewer inserted in the centre comes out clean. Transfer to a wire rack to cool.

To make the icing, pour the lemon juice into a bowl. Gradually sift in the icing sugar, stirring as you go, until smooth, thick and spoonable. Spoon the icing over the cakes and arrange a few pieces of stem ginger on each one. Leave to set before serving. The cakes will keep in an airtight container in the refrigerator for 2–3 days.

strawberry cheesecake cupcakes

Golden vanilla sponge topped with a thick layer of creamy cheesecake-flavoured frosting and decorated with fresh strawberries makes a delicious cupcake. These are best chilled before serving so that the topping sets – but if you just can't wait, they're also good while it's still soft. Top each cake with one big, fat strawberry, or nestle a few halves or tiny ones on top.

115 g unsalted butter, at room temperature

115 g caster sugar

2 eggs, beaten

115 g self-raising flour

½ teaspoon vanilla extract

2 tablespoons whole milk

to decorate:

175 g white chocolate, chopped

175 g cream cheese

6 tablespoons crème fraîche

1½ teaspoons vanilla extract

6 tablespoons icing sugar

fresh strawberries

a 12-hole muffin tin, lined with paper cases

makes 12 cupcakes

Preheat the oven to 180°C (350°F) Gas 4.

Beat the butter and sugar together in a large bowl until pale and fluffy, then beat in the eggs, a little at a time. Sift the flour into the mixture and fold in, then stir in the vanilla extract and milk.

Spoon the mixture into the paper cases. Bake in the preheated oven for about 10 minutes, until risen and golden and a skewer inserted in the centre of a cake comes out clean. Transfer to a wire rack to cool.

To decorate, check if the cakes have risen above the rim of the paper cases. If they have, carefully slice off the top using a serrated knife to create a flat surface. Melt the white chocolate in a heatproof bowl set over a saucepan of simmering water (do not let the bottom of the bowl touch the water), then leave to cool slightly. Beat the cream cheese, crème fraîche, vanilla extract and sifted icing sugar together in a separate bowl, then beat in the melted chocolate. Smooth the mixture over the cakes, then chill for at least 1½ hours until set. Decorate with fresh strawberries and serve. The cakes will keep in an airtight container in the refrigerator for 2 days.

Baking Tip: Bury a vanilla pod in a jar of caster sugar and leave for at least 1 week before use. The sugar will gradually absorb the flavour of the vanilla. Use the vanilla sugar to add extra flavour to cakes, biscuits and desserts or sprinkle it over fresh berries.

lemon, almond and blueberry muffins

Everyone loves a blueberry muffin but these are extra special, packed with ground almonds for a moist, dense texture and with the fresh zestiness of lemon. You can use either fresh or frozen blueberries.

50 g whole blanched almonds

250 g plain flour

1 tablespoon baking powder

85 g golden caster sugar

finely grated zest of 1 lemon

1 large egg

280 ml whole milk

2 teaspoons freshly squeezed lemon juice

4 tablespoons vegetable oil

150 g fresh blueberries, rinsed and thoroughly drained, or frozen blueberries (use straight from the freezer)

a deep 12-hole muffin tin, well greased

makes 12 muffins

Preheat the oven to 200°C (400°F) Gas 6.

Put the almonds in a food processor and process to a coarse meal. They should have more texture than commercially ground almonds. Transfer to a bowl and mix with the sifted flour and baking powder, the sugar and lemon zest.

Lightly beat the egg with the milk, lemon juice and vegetable oil in a small bowl. Add to the dry ingredients and stir just enough to make a coarse, lumpy mixture. Add the blueberries and mix quickly, using as few strokes as possible, leaving the mixture slightly streaky. Do not beat or overmix or the muffins will be tough and dry.

Spoon the mixture into the prepared muffin tin, filling each hole about two-thirds full. Bake in the preheated oven for about 20–25 minutes, until golden and firm to the touch.

Leave to cool in the tin for 1 minute, then turn out onto a wire rack. Eat the same day while still warm, or the next day gently reheated. The muffins can be frozen for up to 1 month.

fresh peach and oat muffins

The addition of fresh peaches is what makes these muffins so special. Serve them warm from the oven for breakfast with good quality raspberry jam and cream cheese, thick Greek-style yoghurt or fromage frais.

115 g rolled oats

300 ml buttermilk

1 large egg, lightly beaten

6 tablespoons melted butter or vegetable oil

85 g light muscovado sugar

200 g plain flour

1 teaspoon baking powder

½ teaspoon bicarbonate of soda

½ teaspoon ground cinnamon

¼ teaspoon ground nutmeg

2 almost ripe, medium peaches, rinsed, stoned and flesh cut into large chunks

a deep 12-hole muffin tin, well greased

makes 12 muffins

Preheat the oven to 220°C (425°F) Gas 7.

Put the rolled oats and buttermilk in a large bowl and leave to soak for 10 minutes. Add the egg, melted butter and sugar to the soaked oat mixture and mix well.

Sift the flour, baking powder, bicarbonate of soda and spices into the oat mixture and stir briefly. Quickly fold in the peaches. Do not beat or overmix; the batter should look slightly streaky. Spoon the mixture into the prepared muffin tin, filling each hole about two-thirds full.

Bake in the preheated oven for about 20–25 minutes, until golden brown and firm to the touch.

Leave to cool in the tin for 1 minute, then turn out onto a wire rack. Eat the same day while still warm, or the next day gently reheated. The muffins can be frozen for up to 1 month.

old-fashioned maple bran muffins

Soured cream is the key to fine-tasting, rich and moist bran muffins and they taste even better if you let the bran mixture soak in the cream for a while before it's baked. To make fruit muffins, replace the pecan nuts with fresh or frozen blueberries or stoned, chopped dates. This recipe makes muffins of a manageable size, not the giants you see in some coffee shops.

225 g soured cream

125 ml whole milk

75 g wheat bran

35 g wheat germ

1 large egg, beaten

4 tablespoons maple syrup

125 g plain flour

1 teaspoon baking powder

½ teaspoon bicarbonate of soda

a pinch of salt

100 g pecan pieces

demerara sugar, for sprinkling

a deep 12-hole muffin tin, lined with paper cases

makes 12 muffins

In a large bowl, combine the soured cream with the milk, then stir in the wheat bran and wheat germ and leave to soak for about 30 minutes.

Meanwhile, preheat the oven to 180°C (350°F) Gas 4.

Stir the egg and maple syrup into the soured cream mixture. Sift the flour, baking powder, bicarbonate of soda and salt into the mixture and mix in. Stir in the pecan pieces.

Spoon the mixture into the paper cases. Sprinkle each muffin with a little demerara sugar, then bake in the preheated oven for about 25 minutes, until firm to the touch.

Carefully turn the muffins out onto a wire rack. Eat the same day while still warm, or the next day gently reheated. The muffins can be frozen for up to 1 month.

Baking Tip: When baking cupcakes or muffins, lightly spray the paper cases with sunflower oil before use. This should make them much easier to peel off the cakes after baking.

chocolate crumble muffins

These delicious chocolate, fruit and nut muffins are a cross between scones, rock cakes and American shortcake. They have a rich, moist texture and are very crumbly. They are best eaten warm so reheat them once they've cooled.

250 g self-raising flour

a pinch of salt

85 g caster sugar

85 g unsalted butter, chilled and cut into cubes

75 g dark chocolate, grated or finely chopped

50 g finely chopped nuts

2 tablespoons very finely chopped mixed peel

1 large egg

about 175 ml single cream

dark chocolate chips or almonds, to decorate

a deep 12-hole muffin tin, lined with paper cases

makes 12 muffins

Preheat the oven to 220°C (425°F) Gas 7.

Sift the flour, salt and sugar into a mixing bowl. Add the cubed butter and, using the tips of your fingers, rub in until the mixture resembles fine breadcrumbs. Stir in the chocolate, nuts and mixed peel. Break the egg into a measuring jug, then add enough cream to make it up to 230 ml. Add the egg mixture to the bowl and mix with a round-bladed knife until the dough comes together – it will be quite sticky.

Divide the mixture between the paper cases, then decorate with chocolate chips or almonds, as preferred.

Bake in the preheated oven for 10 minutes, then reduce the temperature to 180°C (350°F) Gas 4 and bake for a further 5–10 minutes, until golden brown and firm to the touch. Remove from the oven and leave to cool on a wire rack.

Eat the same day while still warm, or the next day gently reheated. The muffins can be frozen for up to 1 month.

layer cakes

fresh pineapple layer cake

A wonderfully exotic recipe from Australia – this moist, fresh fruit cake is packed with flavour. Use a small fresh pineapple or a tin or a plastic tub of ready-prepared fresh pineapple. Leave plain, or decorate with dried banana chips or glacé pineapple chunks.

200 g prepared fresh pineapple

180 g peeled ripe bananas (about 2 small)

250 g self-raising flour

½ teaspoon baking powder

a good pinch of salt

½ teaspoon ground cinnamon

a good pinch of freshly grated nutmeg

225 g light muscovado sugar

2 large eggs, beaten

225 ml sunflower oil

cream cheese frosting:

175 g cream cheese

50 g unsalted butter, at room temperature

150 g icing sugar

1 tablespoon freshly squeezed lemon juice

2 cake tins, 20 cm diameter, greased and base-lined with baking paper

serves 8

Preheat the oven to 180°C (350°F) Gas 4.

Put the pineapple in a food processor and process until fairly finely chopped, or chop with a knife, saving all the juice for another use. Mash the bananas coarsely with a fork.

Sift the flour, baking powder, salt, cinnamon and nutmeg into a large bowl. Mix in the sugar, then make a hollow in the centre.

Put the prepared pineapple and bananas, eggs and oil in the hollow, then mix all the ingredients together with a wooden spoon. When thoroughly combined, divide between the 2 prepared tins and spread evenly.

Bake in the preheated oven for 30–35 minutes until firm to the touch. Leave for a minute, then run a round-bladed knife around the inside edge of the tins to loosen the sponges. Turn out onto a wire rack, peel off the lining paper and leave to cool completely.

To make the frosting, beat the cream cheese and butter together in a bowl with an electric mixer or whisk. Using low speed, beat in the sifted icing sugar, 1 tablespoon at a time. Add lemon juice to taste.

Use the frosting to layer the cakes. Spread about half the frosting on top of one cake. Gently set the second cake on top, then coat the top and sides with the remaining frosting. Serve at room temperature.

Store in an airtight container in a cool cupboard or the refrigerator and eat within 4 days.

chocolate layer cake

Here is a truly fabulous chocolate cake – a delectable combination of moist dark sponge, a fluffy nutty filling and dark chocolate frosting. A handheld electric mixer is essential here, as there is alot of whisking to be done!

55 g cocoa powder

125 ml boiling water

300 g self-raising flour

¼ teaspoon salt

½ teaspoon baking powder

125 g unsalted butter, at room temperature

200 g caster sugar

3 large eggs, beaten

1 teaspoon vanilla extract

100 ml whole milk

nutty filling:

225 ml maple syrup

2 large egg whites

4 tablespoons chopped pecan nuts

chocolate frosting:

3 tablespoons cocoa powder

15 g unsalted butter, at room temperature

1 tablespoon maple syrup

25 ml boiling water

1 egg white

200 g icing sugar

3 cake tins, 20 cm diameter, greased and base-lined with baking paper

serves 12

Sift the cocoa into a heatproof bowl, then stir in the boiling water to make a smooth paste. Let cool.

Preheat the oven to 190°C (375°F) Gas 5.

Sift the flour, salt and baking powder 3 times onto a sheet of greaseproof paper. Put the butter in a bowl and, using an electric mixer, beat until creamy. Beat in the sugar until the mixture is light and fluffy. Gradually beat in the eggs and vanilla extract, then gradually beat in the cooled cocoa mixture. Using a large metal spoon, fold in the flour mixture alternately with the milk. When thoroughly combined, divide the mixture between the 3 prepared tins and spread evenly. Bake in the preheated oven for about 20 minutes, until just firm to the touch. Turn out onto a wire rack, peel off the lining paper and leave to cool completely.

To make the filling, put the maple syrup in a heavy-based saucepan and bring to the boil until it reaches 115°C (238°F) on a sugar thermometer (soft ball stage) – about 5 minutes if you don't have a thermometer. Do take care as the syrup can bubble up alarmingly if the heat is too high. While the syrup is heating, put the egg whites into a clean, grease-free bowl and whisk until stiff peaks form. When the syrup has reached the correct stage, pour it onto the egg whites in a thin steady stream, whisking constantly. Continue whisking until the mixture is very thick and fluffy. Stir in the chopped nuts, then use to sandwich and coat the cakes.

To make the chocolate frosting, sift the cocoa into a heatproof bowl, add the butter and maple syrup, then stir in the boiling water to make a thick, smooth paste. Add the unbeaten egg white, then, using an electric mixer, gradually beat in the sifted icing sugar to make a thin, smooth, spreadable frosting. Pour the frosting over the cake and gently spread it so it covers the entire cake. Chill for a few minutes until firm, then serve at room temperature. Store in an airtight container in a cool cupboard or the refrigerator and eat within 4 days.

banana fudge layer cake

This is a simple vanilla sponge filled with whipped cream, vanilla fudge (home-made or shop-bought) and sliced bananas. Big fans of fudge can decorate the top of the cake with small pieces of extra fudge if liked.

175 g unsalted butter, softened

150 g caster sugar

25 g light muscovado sugar

3 large eggs, at room temperature, beaten

175 g self-raising flour

½ teaspoon vanilla extract

1 tablespoon whole milk

filling and frosting:

300 ml whipping cream, chilled

125 g vanilla fudge, chilled

2 bananas, thinly sliced

extra chopped fudge, to decorate, (optional)

3 cake tins, 20 cm diameter, greased and base-lined with baking paper

serves 12

Preheat the oven to 180°C (350°F) Gas 4.

To make the sponge, put the butter, caster and muscovado sugars, beaten eggs, flour, vanilla extract and milk in a large bowl. Beat at medium speed with an electric mixer or whisk until smooth and thoroughly blended. Divide the mixture between the 3 prepared tins and spread evenly.

Bake in the preheated oven for about 20 minutes, until just firm to the touch. Leave to cool for 1 minute, then run a round-bladed knife inside the rim of the tins just to loosen the sponges. Turn out onto a wire rack, peel off the lining paper and leave to cool completely.

To assemble, put the cream in a chilled bowl and whip until soft peaks form. Grate the fudge onto the cream and stir in. Set one layer of sponge on a serving plate, spread with a third of the cream and cover with half the banana slices. Top with another layer of sponge and spread with half the remaining cream, top with the rest of the bananas, then finally add the last layer of sponge. Spread the remaining cream on top of the cake and decorate with extra chopped fudge, if liked.

Keep cool and eat the same day, or store in an airtight container in the refrigerator and eat within 2 days.

maple syrup pecan layer cake

An elegant, mile-high, three-layer sponge cake, feather-light but full of rich flavours. This cake is very delicate and cuts best the next day so make it ahead if you plan to serve it for a birthday or a special occasion.

350 g unsalted butter, at room temperature

280 g caster sugar

4 large eggs, lightly beaten

3 tablespoons pure maple syrup

120 g pecan nuts, finely chopped (in a food processor), but not ground

350 g self-raising flour

a pinch of salt

maple frosting:

225 ml pure maple syrup

2 large egg whites

pecan halves, to decorate

3 cake tins, 20 cm diameter, greased and base-lined with baking paper

serves 12

Preheat the oven to 180°C (350°F) Gas 4.

Using an electric mixer, beat the butter in a bowl until lighter in colour, then add the sugar, a spoonful at a time, while still beating. When all the sugar has been added, scrape down the sides of the bowl, then beat until the mixture is very light and fluffy. Beat in the eggs a spoonful at a time, then gradually beat in the maple syrup. Add the pecans, sifted flour and salt to the bowl and, using a large metal spoon or rubber spatula, gently fold into the mixture.

Divide the mixture between the prepared tins and spread evenly. Bake in the preheated oven for 25–30 minutes, until golden and springy to the touch. Leave to cool for a minute, then run a round-bladed knife around the inside edge of the tins to loosen the sponges. Carefully turn out onto a wire rack, peel off the lining paper and leave to cool completely.

Meanwhile, to make the frosting, heat the maple syrup in a heavy-based saucepan and let boil gently until it reaches 115°C (238°F) on a sugar thermometer (soft ball stage) – about 5 minutes if you don't have a thermometer. Do take care as the syrup can bubble up alarmingly if the heat is too high. While the syrup is heating, whisk the egg whites in a clean, grease-free bowl until stiff peaks form using an electric mixer or whisk. Pour the hot syrup onto the egg whites in a thin stream while still whisking constantly. Keep whisking for a further 1 minute or until the frosting is very thick and fluffy.

When the cakes are completely cold, use the frosting to layer them. Spread about one-sixth of the mixture on top of one cake. Gently set a second cake on top and spread with another one-sixth of the frosting. Top with the last cake, then coat the top and side with the rest of the frosting. Decorate the top with pecan halves.

Store in an airtight container in a cool cupboard or the refrigerator and eat within 4 days.

victoria sandwich with strawberries & cream

A classic Victoria sandwich filled with cream and fresh strawberries makes a wonderful centrepiece for a traditional afternoon tea. Make it in summer when strawberries are in season and at their juicy and fragrant best.

180 g unsalted butter, at room temperature

180 g caster sugar

3 eggs

180 g self-raising flour

3½ tablespoons good-quality strawberry jam

140 g strawberries, hulled and halved or quartered, depending on size

120 ml whipping cream

icing sugar, for dusting

2 cake tins, 20 cm diameter, greased and base-lined with baking paper

serves 8

Preheat the oven to 180°C (350°F) Gas 4.

Beat the butter and caster sugar together in a large bowl until pale and fluffy. Beat in the eggs one at a time. Sift the flour into the mixture and fold in until thoroughly combined.

Spoon the mixture into the prepared tins and spread out evenly. Bake in the preheated oven for 20–25 minutes until golden brown and the sponges spring back when pressed gently. Turn out onto a wire rack, gently peel off the lining paper and leave to cool completely.

To serve, cut a thin slice off of the top of one of the cakes to create a flat surface. Spread the strawberry jam on top and top with the strawberries. Whip the cream in a bowl until it stands in soft peaks, then spread on top of the strawberries. Top with the second cake, press down gently and dust with sifted icing sugar.

Keep cool and eat the same day, or store in an airtight container in the refrigerator and eat within 2 days.

Baking Tip: When whipping cream, chill the bowl and whisk before-hand and make sure the cream's well chilled too. Use a balloon whisk rather than electric beaters – the cream will take a little longer to whip but there is less chance of overwhipping, for which there is no remedy.

snow-topped coconut cake

This light and fluffy coconut cake is topped with a creamy frosting that has a refreshing tang of lime. It's snowy white appearance makes it a pretty alternative to the more traditional festive fruit cake.

40 g creamed coconut

140 g unsalted butter

175 g caster sugar

3 eggs

150 g self-raising flour

40 g desiccated coconut

finely grated zest of 1 lime

lime frosting:

225 g cream cheese

75 g icing sugar

1 tablespoon freshly squeezed lime juice

40 g soft coconut flakes

2 cake tins, 20 cm diameter, greased and base-lined with baking paper

serves 8

Preheat the oven to 180°C (350°F) Gas 4.

Put the creamed coconut in a bowl and soften with a wooden spoon. Add the butter and sugar and beat together until pale and fluffy. Beat in the eggs, one at a time. Sift in the flour and fold it in, then stir in the desiccated coconut and lime zest.

Spoon the mixture into the prepared tins and level the surface. Bake in the preheated oven for 20–25 minutes, until golden brown and a skewer inserted in the centre comes out clean. Turn the cakes out onto a wire rack, peel off the lining paper and leave to cool completely.

To make the frosting, beat the cream cheese, icing sugar and lime juice together in a bowl. Place one of the cakes on a serving plate. Spread slightly less than half of the frosting on top of the cake, then place the second cake on top. Spread over the remaining frosting and scatter with coconut flakes.

Keep cool and eat the same day, or store in an airtight container in the refrigerator and eat within 2 days.

Baking Tip: If a cake recipe requires the juice and zest from a citrus fruit, finely grate off the zest first (you can freeze any you don't need in an ice-cube tray for future use) before squeezing out the juice.

✓ spicy carrot and pistachio cake

There's something comforting and homely about carrot cake, making it the perfect indulgent treat for any coffee morning or afternoon tea. This recipe has a dense, moist crumb and a lemony cream cheese frosting.

225 g self-raising flour

1 teaspoon baking powder

1 teaspoon ground cinnamon

½ teaspoon ground ginger

¼ teaspoon freshly grated nutmeg

150 ml sunflower oil

3 eggs

200 g light soft brown sugar

350 g grated carrots

finely grated zest of 1 orange

60 g roasted, unsalted pistachio nuts, roughly chopped

lemon frosting:

200 g cream cheese

75 g icing sugar

1½ teaspoons freshly squeezed lemon juice

finely grated zest of 1 lemon

chopped unsalted pistachio nuts, to decorate

crystallized violets (optional)

a cake tin, 20 cm diameter, greased and base-lined

serves 8–12

Preheat the oven to 180°C (350°F) Gas 4.

Sift the flour, baking powder and spices into a large bowl and make a well in the centre. In a separate bowl, beat the sunflower oil, eggs and sugar together. Pour this mixture into the dry ingredients and fold together.

Add the grated carrot, orange zest and nuts and mix well to combine. Spoon the mixture into the prepared tin and level the surface. Bake in the preheated oven for about 1 hour, or until a skewer inserted in the centre comes out clean. Leave to cool in the tin for 10 minutes, then turn out onto a wire rack, peel off the lining paper and leave to cool completely.

To make the frosting, beat the cream cheese, icing sugar, lemon juice and zest together in a bowl until smooth and creamy. Spread over the cooled cake, then decorate with pistachios and crystallized violets, if using.

Keep cool and eat the same day, or store in an airtight container in the refrigerator and eat within 2 days.

coffee and walnut cake

This classic sponge cake is enduringly popular, perhaps because something magical happens when coffee and walnuts come together.

180 g unsalted butter,
at room temperature

180 g caster sugar

3 eggs

180 g self-raising flour

60 g walnut pieces

2 teaspoons instant coffee
granules, dissolved in
1 tablespoon hot water

walnut halves, to decorate

coffee frosting:

250 g mascarpone cheese

85 g icing sugar

1 teaspoon instant coffee
granules, dissolved in
2 teaspoons hot water

2 cake tins, 20 cm diameter,
greased and base-lined

serves 8–12

Preheat the oven to 180°C (350°F) Gas 4.

Put the butter and sugar in a large bowl and cream together until pale and fluffy. Beat in the eggs one at a time. Sift the flour into the butter mixture and stir to combine. Fold in the walnut pieces and coffee. Divide the cake mixture between the two prepared tins and level the surface.

Bake in the preheated oven for 20–25 minutes, until golden and the sponges spring back when gently pressed or a skewer inserted in the centre comes out clean. Turn out onto a wire rack, peel off the lining paper and leave to cool completely.

To make the frosting, beat the mascarpone, sifted icing sugar and coffee together until smooth and creamy. Spread slightly less than half the frosting over one of the cooled cakes, then place the second cake on top. Spread the remaining frosting over the top and decorate with walnut halves to finish.

Keep cool and eat the same day, or store in an airtight container in the refrigerator and eat within 2 days.

angel food cake

This pure white, whisked sponge cake is the classic all-American cake. It's traditionally baked in a ring-shaped tin and tastes divine served with fresh blueberries or juicy wedges of ripe peach on the side.

125 g plain flour

250 g caster sugar

10 egg whites

1 teaspoon cream of tartar

½ teaspoon vanilla extract

a punnet of fresh blueberries or 6 ripe peaches stoned and sliced, to serve

angel frosting:

115 g caster sugar

2 egg whites

2 teaspoons golden syrup

½ teaspoon vanilla extract

a ring mould, 25 cm diameter, or a non-stick cake tin, 20 cm diameter, lightly greased

serves 8–12

Preheat the oven to 180°C (350°F) Gas 4.

In a large bowl, sift together the flour and half the caster sugar three times, until very light. Set aside.

In a separate, grease-free bowl, whisk the egg whites with the cream of tartar until stiff, then gradually whisk in the remaining sugar until the mixture is thick and glossy. Whisk in the vanilla extract.

Sift half the flour and sugar mixture into the egg whites and gently fold in, then sift in the remaining flour and sugar mixture and fold in.

Spoon the mixture into the prepared ring mould and bake in the preheated oven for about 40 minutes, until a skewer inserted into the cake comes out clean. Turn out onto a wire rack and leave to cool completely.

To make the frosting, put the sugar in a small, heavy-based saucepan with 4 tablespoons water and heat, stirring constantly, until the sugar dissolves, then let it boil gently until it reaches 115°C (238°F) on a sugar thermometer (softball stage) – about 5 minutes if you don't have a thermometer.

In a clean, grease-free bowl, whisk the egg whites until very stiff, then gradually pour the sugar syrup into the egg whites in a thin stream, whisking constantly until thick and glossy. Whisk in the golden syrup and vanilla extract and continue whisking until the frosting has cooled. Use a palette knife to spread it over the cooled cake. Serve with blueberries or slices of fresh peach, as preferred.

Keep cool and eat the same day, or store in an airtight container in the refrigerator and eat within 2 days.

dark chocolate floral cake

This rich chocolate sponge covered in dark, glossy frosting and decorated with crystallized flower petals, makes a stunning cake for any special occasion. Serve it just as it is, or with chilled whipped cream on the side.

100 g dark chocolate

125 g unsalted butter, at room temperature

170 g caster sugar

2 eggs, separated

170 g self-raising flour

1 tablespoon cocoa powder

60 ml whole milk

crystallized violets, to decorate

dark chocolate frosting:

200 g dark chocolate, chopped

200 ml double cream

a springform cake tin, 20 cm diameter, greased and base-lined

serves 8–12

Preheat the oven to 180°C (350°F) Gas 4.

Melt the chocolate in a heatproof bowl set over a saucepan of gently simmering water (do not let the bottom of the bowl touch the water). Remove from the heat and set aside.

Put the butter and sugar in a large bowl and beat to combine, then beat in the egg yolks. Fold in the melted chocolate, then sift in the flour and cocoa powder and mix to combine. Stir in the milk, a little at a time, to loosen the mixture.

In a clean, grease-free bowl, whisk the egg whites until stiff, then fold into the chocolate mixture, about a quarter at a time. Spoon the mixture into the prepared tin and level the surface. Bake in the preheated oven for about 45 minutes, until a skewer inserted in the centre comes out clean. Turn out onto a wire rack, peel off the lining paper and leave to cool completely.

To make the frosting, put the chocolate in a heatproof bowl, then put the cream in a saucepan and heat until almost boiling. Pour the hot cream over the chocolate and stir until melted. Leave to thicken for 10–15 minutes, then spread over the top and side of the cake with a palette knife. Sprinkle with crystallized violets and let the frosting set.

Keep cool and eat the same day, or store in an airtight container in the refrigerator and eat within 2 days.

Baking Tip: Keep chocolate dry when melting it, a single drop of water or steam will cause it to 'seize'. If it becomes stiff and grainy take it off the heat and stir in vegetable oil, a few drops at a time, until the chocolate is smooth. However, if the chocolate is very scorched it may be unusable.

carrot and walnut cake

This tempting cake is crumbly and soft and probably best eaten with a spoon! If you are nervous about cutting this rather fragile cake through the centre, simply spread the filling over the top of the cooled cake instead.

2 eggs, separated

110 g raw (unrefined) sugar

200 ml light olive oil

1 teaspoon bicarbonate of soda

185 g plain flour

2 teaspoons baking powder

1 teaspoon ground cinnamon

¼ teaspoon freshly grated nutmeg

200 g grated carrots

100 g walnut halves

filling:

250 g cream cheese

125 g unsalted butter, cut into cubes

3 tablespoons light soft brown sugar

2–3 tablespoons maple syrup

a springform cake tin, 20 cm diameter, lightly greased

serves 8

Preheat the oven to 180°C (350°F) Gas 4.

Put the egg yolks and sugar in a large bowl and beat together. Add the olive oil and bicarbonate of soda and beat until just combined. Fold in the flour, baking powder, spices, carrots and walnuts until combined. The mixture should be thick.

In a separate grease-free bowl, whisk the egg whites with an electric mixer until they form soft peaks. Fold them into the cake mixture in 2 batches. Spoon into the prepared tin and level the surface. Bake in the preheated oven for about 45–50 minutes, until golden and slightly puffed. Leave to cool in the tin for about 10 minutes before turning it out onto a wire rack and leave to cool completely.

To make the filling, put the cream cheese and butter in a bowl and leave them to come to room temperature. Add the sugar and, using an electric mixer, beat for 5 minutes, until there are no lumps and the beaters leave a trail when turned off. Add the maple syrup a little at a time and beat for a further 2 minutes, until the mixture is smooth and a spreadable consistency.

Carefully slice the cooled cake in half and spread the filling on the bottom layer. Replace the top of the cake.

Keep cool and eat the same day, or store in an airtight container in the refrigerator and eat within 2 days.

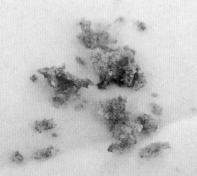

everyday cakes

lemon drizzle cake

Sometimes it's the plain cakes that are the best. This one is wonderfully buttery and zesty and is delicious served simply, cut into little squares. To achieve a really crisp, sugary crust on top, combine the sugar and lemon juice at the last minute and pour straight over the cake before letting it cool.

140 g unsalted butter, at room temperature

140 g caster sugar

2 large eggs

finely grated zest of 1 lemon

140 g self-raising flour

lemony topping:

4 tablespoons caster sugar

freshly squeezed juice of 1 lemon

a loose-bottomed cake tin, 20 cm square, greased and base-lined with baking paper

makes 12 squares

Preheat oven to 180°C (350°F) Gas 4.

Beat the butter and sugar together in a large bowl until pale and creamy. Beat in the eggs, one at a time, then stir in the lemon zest. Sift the flour into the mixture and fold in until well combined. Spoon the mixture into the prepared tin and level the surface. Bake in the preheated oven for about 20 minutes, until well risen and golden and a skewer inserted in the centre comes out clean.

Transfer the cake tin to a wire rack and prick the top of the cake all over using the skewer. Sprinkle the top of the cake with 1 tablespoon of the sugar for the topping. Quickly combine the remaining sugar and lemon juice in a small bowl and immediately pour it over the top of the cake. Leave to cool in the tin, then carefully unmould and peel off the lining paper. Cut into small squares to serve.

Store in an airtight container in a cool cupboard or the refrigerator and eat within 3 days.

blueberry lemon pound cake

This classic pound cake recipe (known as *quatre quarts* in France and *sandkuchen* in Germany), uses equal weights of butter, flour, sugar and eggs and needs plenty of beating to add air and lightness.

250 g unsalted butter, at room temperature

250 g caster sugar

finely grated zest of 1 lemon

4 eggs, at room temperature

a pinch of salt

250 g self-raising flour

75 g soft dried blueberries

icing sugar, for dusting

a cake tin, 27 x 18 cm, well greased

makes 8–12 squares

Preheat the oven to 180°C (350°F) Gas 4.

Put the butter in the bowl of a free-standing electric mixer and beat at low speed until creamy. Increase the speed and gradually beat in the sugar, followed by the lemon zest.

Put the eggs and salt in a jug, beat lightly, then add to the creamed mixture, 1 tablespoon at a time, beating well after each addition. Add 1 tablespoon flour with the 2 last portions of egg to prevent the mixture from separating.

Toss the blueberries with a little of the remaining flour and set aside. Sift the rest of the flour into the mixture and gently fold in with a large metal spoon. When you no longer see streaks of flour, mix in the blueberries.

Spoon the mixture into the prepared tin and level the surface. Bake in the preheated oven for about 40 minutes, or until a skewer inserted in the centre comes out clean.

Leave to cool in the tin for 10 minutes, then carefully turn out onto a wire rack and leave to cool completely. Dust liberally with sifted icing sugar before serving. Store in an airtight container in a cool cupboard and eat within 3 days.

Baking Tip: Toss dried fruit, glacé cherries or nuts in a little flour or ground almonds before adding them to a cake mixture. This should stop the fruit or nuts sinking to the bottom of the cake and keep them evenly dispersed during baking.

thanksgiving cranberry bundt

This cake is a New England classic, where cranberries grow in abundance, and is often served at Thanksgiving. It makes a great centrepiece for any festive occasion when made in a traditional 'bundt' cake tin, as shown here.

110 g unsalted butter, at room temperature

2 large eggs, at room temperature, beaten

160 g light muscovado sugar

225 ml soured cream

40 g finely chopped almonds

325 g plain flour

1 teaspoon ground cinnamon

½ teaspoon bicarbonate of soda

1 teaspoon baking powder

icing sugar, for dusting

filling:

60 g whole blanched almonds

150 g fresh cranberries

2 teaspoons ground cinnamon

85 g light muscovado sugar

a Bundt tin, 23 cm diameter, well greased, or a 900 g loaf tin, greased and lined with baking paper

serves 8–12

Preheat the oven to 180°C (350°F) Gas 4.

Make the filling first. Put the almonds into a food processor and chop finely to make a coarse powder (rather than using shop-bought finely ground almonds). Transfer to a large bowl. Put the cranberries in the processor and chop coarsely. Add to the almonds, then add the cinnamon and sugar and mix well. Set aside until needed.

Put the soft butter, beaten eggs, sugar, soured cream and chopped almonds in a large bowl. Beat with an electric mixer or whisk on medium speed until very smooth. Sift the flour, cinnamon, bicarbonate of soda and baking powder into the mixture, then stir in with a large metal spoon. When thoroughly mixed, spoon half the mixture into the prepared tin. Sprinkle the cranberry filling over the mixture, then top with the rest of the cake mixture.

Bake in the preheated oven for about 50 minutes, or until a skewer inserted in the thickest part of the cake comes out clean. Leave to cool in the tin for 15 minutes, then carefully turn out onto a wire rack, dust with icing sugar and leave to cool completely. Store in an airtight container in a cool cupboard and eat within 4 days.

lime and blueberry cake with lime syrup

Cooking brings out the flavour of blueberries, which can be a rather uneventful fruit when eaten raw. Here, they pepper a light butter cake flavoured with lime zest, then the whole thing is drenched in lime syrup, which soaks into the sponge to add flavour and moistness.

225 g unsalted butter, softened

225 g golden caster sugar

4 eggs, beaten

225 g self-raising flour, sifted with a pinch of salt

200 g blueberries

finely grated zest of 2 limes

30 g ground almonds

1–2 teaspoons freshly squeezed lime juice

lime syrup:

finely grated zest of 1 lime

freshly squeezed juice of 4 limes

125 g golden caster sugar

a cake tin, 20–23 cm square, buttered and lined

makes 12 squares

Preheat the oven to 180°C (350°F) Gas 4.

Put the butter and sugar in a large bowl and cream together until light and fluffy. Gradually beat in the eggs, adding a little of the flour towards the end to prevent curdling. Toss the blueberries with 1 tablespoon of the remaining flour and set aside. Beat the lime zest into the cake mixture, then fold in the remaining flour and almonds. Fold in 1–2 teaspoons lime juice to give you a good dropping consistency – the mixture should drop easily from the spoon when tapped.

Fold in most of the blueberries (about 150 g) and spoon the mixture into the prepared cake tin. Level the surface, then sprinkle with the remaining fruit (which will sink as the cake rises). Bake in the preheated oven for about 40–45 minutes, or until firm when gently touched in the centre.

While the cake is cooking, make the lime syrup. Put the lime zest and juice in a small, heavy-based saucepan with the sugar and heat gently, stirring continuously. Do not let it bubble – just heat slightly, leaving a slight graininess. As soon as the cake comes out of the oven, prick it all over with a skewer, then spoon over the syrup. Leave the cake to cool in the tin. Cut into squares to serve.

Store in an airtight container in a cool cupboard and eat within 4 days.

soured cream coffee cake

A coffee cake in name only – this dark, spicy cake is meant to be enjoyed with a cup of mid-morning coffee. It is best eaten warm so serve freshly-baked or wrap in foil and reheat gently for a few minutes in a low oven.

115 g unsalted butter, at room temperature

170 g light muscovado sugar

250 g plain flour

2 teaspoons bicarbonate of soda

2 large eggs

250 ml soured cream

filling and topping:

3 tablespoons dark muscovado sugar

1 tablespoon ground cinnamon

90 g walnut pieces

a 1-kg loaf tin, greased and base-lined with baking paper

serves 8–12

Preheat the oven to 180°C (350°F) Gas 4.

Using an electric mixer or a wooden spoon, beat the butter until light and creamy. Add the sugar and beat again until light and fluffy. Sift the flour and bicarbonate of soda into the creamed butter mixture. Stir once or twice, then quickly beat the eggs with the soured cream and add to the bowl. Using a rubber spatula or wooden spoon, stir all the ingredients together to make a soft, smooth mixture.

Mix the filling and topping ingredients together in a separate bowl. Spoon half the cake mixture into the prepared loaf tin, then sprinkle over half the filling and topping mixture. Spoon the rest of the cake mixture on top and level the surface. Sprinkle over the rest of the filling and topping mixture, then press lightly onto the surface of the loaf.

Bake in the preheated oven for about 45–60 minutes, until lightly browned and firm and a skewer inserted in the centre comes out clean. Leave to cool in the tin for 5 minutes, then carefully turn out onto a wire rack and peel off the lining paper. Serve warm. Store in an airtight container in a cool cupboard and eat within 3 days.

upside-down peach cake

You can use either yellow or white peaches here. Yellow peaches have a more robust flavour and the white ones a more subtle flavour that is more like that of nectarines. Look out for big, juicy summer peaches and try to resist eating them before you make this delicious cake!

4 large fresh peaches

125 g unsalted butter, softened

185 g light soft brown sugar

3 eggs, separated

185 g self-raising flour

250 g soured cream

icing sugar, for dusting

single cream, to serve (optional)

a springform cake tin,
23 cm diameter, base-lined
and lightly greased

serves 8

Preheat the oven to 180°C (350°F) Gas 4.

Halve the peaches, discard the stones, then cut each half in half again. Arrange the peach quarters on the bottom of the prepared cake tin and set aside until needed.

Put the butter and sugar in a large bowl and beat together with an electric mixer until the sugar has completely dissolved and the mixture is caramel-coloured. Add the egg yolks, 1 at a time, beating for 1 minute between each addition. Fold the flour and soured cream through the cake mixture in 2 batches.

In a separate grease-free bowl, whisk the egg whites with an electric whisk until they form firm peaks. Using a large metal spoon, fold the whites into the cake mixture in 2 batches. Spoon the mixture over the peaches and bake in the preheated oven for 40–45 minutes, until the top of the cake is golden and the centre springs back when gently pressed.

Leave to cool in the tin for 10 minutes, then carefully turn out and peel off the lining paper. Dust with icing sugar and serve warm with single cream for pouring, if liked.

Baking Tip: To make ordinary cream into soured cream, stir 1–2 teaspoons of freshly squeezed lemon juice into 150 ml fresh single cream. Leave it to stand and the cream will thicken within 15–30 minutes and can be used as a substitute for soured cream in most recipes.

strawberry buttermilk cake

This is a smooth, dense cake given a light and creamy crumb by using buttermilk. It can be made in a conventional round cake tin or baked in a rectangular tin and cut into squares to serve.

250 g self-raising flour

225 g caster sugar

125 g unsalted butter, softened

2 large eggs

225 g buttermilk

375 g strawberries, hulled

single cream, to serve

crumble topping:

40 g plain flour

50 g unsalted butter, chilled and cut into cubes

95 g light soft brown sugar

a cake tin, 20 cm diameter, greased and lined

serves 6–8

Preheat the oven to 180°C (350°F) Gas 4.

Put the flour and sugar in a bowl and mix. Put the butter, eggs and buttermilk in a food processor and process until smooth. With the motor running, add the flour and sugar mixture and process until well combined. Scrape down the sides of the mixer bowl to evenly incorporate all the ingredients and stir in the strawberries. Spoon the mixture into the prepared cake tin and level the surface.

To make the crumble topping, put the flour and butter in a bowl and, using the tips of your fingers, rub the butter into the flour until the mixture resembles coarse breadcrumbs. Stir in the sugar.

Evenly sprinkle the topping mixture over the cake and bake in the preheated oven for 50 minutes, until golden brown on top.

Leave the cake to cool in the tin before cutting into squares and serving with cream. Store in an airtight container in a cool cupboard or the refrigerator and eat within 2 days.

pear and ginger crumble cake

This is a deliciously spicy cake with a very moreish texture. Ground ginger loses its intensity if left sitting in the storecupboard for too long, so do make sure that what you use here is not past it's use-by date. You could try this recipe substituting apples for pears and ground cinnamon for the ginger.

125 g unsalted butter, softened

125 g golden caster sugar

2 eggs, at room temperature

125 g plain flour

2 teaspoons baking powder

2 firm pears, peeled, cored and sliced

1 tablespoon freshly squeezed lemon juice

thick double cream, to serve

ginger crumble topping:

60 g plain flour

1 teaspoon ground ginger

50 g cold unsalted butter, cut into cubes

3 tablespoons light soft brown sugar

a springform cake tin, 20 cm diameter, base-lined and lightly greased

serves 8

Preheat the oven to 180°C (350°F) Gas 4.

First make the crumble topping. Put the flour and ginger in a bowl. Add the cold butter and quickly rub it into the flour using your fingertips. Add the sugar and rub again until the mixture resembles coarse sand. Refrigerate until needed.

Beat the softened butter and sugar together in a bowl with an electric mixer until pale and creamy. Add the eggs, 1 at a time, and beat well between each addition. Tip in the flour and baking powder and beat for 1 minute, until the mixture is smooth and well combined. Spoon the mixture into the prepared cake tin and level the surface. Toss the pears in a bowl with the lemon juice and arrange them on top of the cake. Sprinkle the crumble topping over the top and bake in the preheated oven for 40–45 minutes, until the cake is risen and golden on top.

Leave to cool slightly before removing from the tin and cutting into slices. Serve warm with a dollop of cream. Store in an airtight container in a cool cupboard or the refrigerator and eat within 2 days.

black and white chocolate marble loaf cake

It's very easy to turn a basic pound cake mixture into an impressive, richly flavoured marbled loaf. For a real treat, serve slices of warm cake for pudding with plenty of whipped cream or hot custard.

225 g unsalted butter,
at room temperature

225 g golden caster sugar

4 large eggs, at room
temperature, lightly beaten

1 teaspoon vanilla extract

225 g self-raising flour

75 g dark chocolate, chopped

1 tablespoon cocoa powder

75 g white chocolate, chopped

whipped cream or custard,
to serve (optional)

a 900-g loaf tin, greased and
base-lined with baking paper

serves 8–12

Preheat the oven to 180°C (350°F) Gas 4.

Put the butter in a large mixing bowl and, using a wooden spoon or electric mixer, beat until very creamy. Beat in the sugar and continue beating for about 2 minutes until the mixture is lighter in colour and consistency. Gradually beat in the eggs, then beat in the vanilla extract. Sift the flour into the creamed mixture and gently fold in with a large metal spoon.

Spoon half the cake mixture into another mixing bowl. Put the dark chocolate in a heatproof bowl set over a saucepan of simmering but not boiling water and melt gently (do not let the base of the bowl touch the water). Remove the bowl from the heat and leave to cool. Sift the cocoa onto one portion of cake mixture, add the cooled melted dark chocolate, then, using a large metal spoon, fold in until evenly mixed.

Put the white chocolate in a separate heatproof bowl set over a saucepan of simmering but not boiling water and melt gently (do not let the base of the bowl touch the water). Remove the bowl from the heat and leave to cool. Using a large metal spoon, fold into the remaining cake mixture.

Spoon both cake mixtures into the prepared tin, using each mixture alternately. To make the marbling, draw a knife through the mixtures and swirl together.

Bake in the preheated oven for about 1¼ hours, until a skewer inserted in the centre comes out clean. Turn out onto a wire rack, peel off the lining paper and leave to cool completely.

Store in an airtight container in a cool cupboard and eat within 5 days.

breakfast tea loaf

This traditional tea loaf should be served thickly sliced, warm or even toasted, with or without butter and jam. For a full tea-flavour, use a good strong variety such as a breakfast or Irish blend, or a rich malty Assam.

100 g shredded bran cereal

120 g dark muscovado sugar

130 g mixed dried fruit

175 ml strong brewed tea, warm

30 g walnut pieces

100 g plain flour, sifted

1½ teaspoons baking powder

1½ teaspoons mixed spice

a 450-g loaf tin, greased and base-lined with baking paper

serves 8

Put the bran, sugar and dried fruit in a large bowl, add the tea, stir well, then cover and leave to soak for 30 minutes.

Add the remaining ingredients to the bran mixture and stir with a wooden spoon until thoroughly mixed. (The bran will disappear into the mixture.)

Preheat the oven to 180°C (350°F) Gas 4.

Spoon the mixture into the prepared loaf tin and level the surface. Bake in the preheated oven for about 45 minutes, until firm and well risen and a skewer inserted in the centre comes out clean.

Leave the loaf to cool in the tin until lukewarm, then turn out onto a wire rack and leave to cool completely. The tea loaf is best if wrapped in baking paper and kept for 1 day before cutting. Store in an airtight container in a cool cupboard and eat within 4 days.

carrot and almond loaf cake

Everyone loves a carrot cake – this one is moist and packed with creamy, crunchy almonds. Serve it plain or spread with cream cheese for a delicious breakfast or teatime treat.

100 g self-raising flour

300 g ground almonds

50 g whole blanched almonds, very coarsely ground, or flaked almonds

finely grated zest of 1 lemon

250 g carrots, peeled and grated

6 large eggs, separated

200 g light muscovado sugar

a 1-kg loaf tin, greased and base-lined with baking paper

serves 8–12

Preheat the oven to 180°C (350°F) Gas 4.

Put the sifted flour, all the almonds, lemon zest and carrots in a large bowl and mix well with a wooden spoon.

Whisk the egg yolks with half the sugar in a separate bowl until very thick and fluffy. In another, spotlessly clean, grease-free bowl, whisk the egg whites until stiff peaks form, then gradually whisk in the remaining sugar to form a meringue mixture. Using a large metal spoon, gently fold the carrot mixture into the whisked yolk mixture, followed by the meringue. (There should be no trace of meringue visible in the mixture.)

Spoon the mixture into the prepared loaf tin and level the surface. Bake in the preheated oven for about 1 hour until golden and firm to the touch and a skewer inserted in the centre comes out clean. Leave the cake to cool in the tin until lukewarm, then turn out onto a wire rack. Peel off the lining paper and leave to cool completely. Store in an airtight container in a cool cupboard and eat within 2 days.

Baking Tip: To coarsely grind nuts to use as a baking ingredient, process them in a food processor until they are the consistency of fine breadcrumbs. Be careful not to overprocess them though, or you may end up with nut butter.

old-fashioned blueberry gingerbread

Blueberries, fresh or frozen, are now available all year round. They add a good sharp bite to this richly flavoured gingerbread loaf. Unlike most gingerbreads, which improve on keeping, this fresh fruit version is best eaten straightaway.

150 g blueberries, fresh or straight from the freezer

225 g plain flour

1 teaspoon bicarbonate of soda

a good pinch of salt

1 tablespoon ground ginger

1 teaspoon ground cinnamon

1 teaspoon ground mixed spice

100 g light muscovado sugar

100 g unsalted butter

100 g black treacle

100 g golden syrup

1 large egg

285 ml buttermilk

a 900-g loaf tin, greased and base-lined with baking paper

serves 8–12

Preheat the oven to 180°C (350°F) Gas 4.

Toss the blueberries in 1 tablespoon of the measured flour and set aside. Sift the rest of the flour, the bicarbonate of soda, salt, all the spices and the sugar into a large bowl.

Gently melt the butter with the black treacle and golden syrup in a small saucepan set over low heat. In a separate bowl, whisk the egg and buttermilk together until just mixed.

Add the butter mixture to the flour mixture, then add the egg mixture. Mix thoroughly with a wooden spoon to make a smooth mixture. Pour the mixture into the prepared loaf tin, then scatter the blueberries evenly over the top.

Bake in the preheated oven for 45–55 minutes, until firm to the touch and a skewer inserted in the centre of the loaf comes out clean.

Set the tin on a wire rack and leave the gingerbread to cool before removing. Store in an airtight container in a cool cupboard and eat within 2 days. This gingerbread doesn't freeze very well.

chocolate and banana bread

This is a real treat for children everywhere or the big kid in all of us. Use milk chocolate and a banana- or chocolate-flavoured yoghurt for children or really dark chocolate and natural yoghurt for adults. This bread really does improve with keeping – even for just a day.

55 g unsalted butter, softened

150 g light soft brown sugar

2 large eggs, beaten

100 g natural yoghurt, or banana- or chocolate-flavoured yoghurt

350 g bananas, peeled and mashed

300 g self-raising flour

½ teaspoon salt

200 g dark chocolate or milk chocolate (over 32% cocoa solids), coarsely grated

chocolate and hazelnut spread, such as Nutella, to serve (optional)

2 x 450-g loaf tins, greased, base-lined with baking paper and lightly dusted with flour

makes 2 large loaves

Preheat the oven to 180°C (350°F) Gas 4.

Beat the butter and sugar together in a bowl using an electric mixer until well combined. Gradually whisk in the eggs, little by little, then the yoghurt, and finally stir in the mashed bananas. Fold in the sifted flour and salt, followed by the grated chocolate. Spoon the mixture into the prepared loaf tins and level the surface of both.

Bake in the preheated oven for about 35 minutes, or until risen and firm and a metal skewer inserted into the centre of a loaf comes out clean. Leave to cool in the tins for 10 minutes, then turn out onto a wire rack, peel off the lining paper and leave to cool completely.

The loaves are best if wrapped in baking paper and kept for 1 day before cutting. Store in an airtight container in a cool cupboard and eat within 4 days. Serve in thick slices with chocolate and hazelnut spread, if liked.

> *Baking Tip: If you are creaming butter and sugar together or beating butter for a cake mixture and it is slightly too cold to mix easily, wrap a warm, damp tea towel around the mixing bowl and continue to beat the butter – the warmth will help the ingredients to blend better.*

apple-topped loaf cake

This moist apple cake tastes every bit as delicious as it looks. It makes a scrumptious dessert with some vanilla ice cream, but is also good for tucking into a lunchbox or picnic hamper.

150 g unsalted butter, melted

150 g caster sugar

2 eggs, beaten

150 g ground almonds

50 g plain flour

1 teaspoon baking powder

finely grated zest of 1 lemon

100 ml whole milk

2 red eating apples, halved, cored and thinly sliced

icing sugar, to dust

a 450-g loaf tin, greased and base-lined with baking paper

Preheat the oven to 150°C (300°F) Gas 2.

Beat the butter and sugar together in a large bowl with an electric whisk until smooth, light and fluffy. Add the eggs, a little at a time, stirring well between each addition.

Stir in the almonds, flour and baking powder, then stir in the lemon zest and milk. Spoon the mixture into the prepared loaf tin and level the surface. Arrange the apple slices evenly over the top.

Bake in the preheated oven for about 45 minutes, until the cake has risen and is golden and springy to the touch. Leave to cool in the tin for 20 minutes, then turn out onto a wire rack, peel off the lining paper and leave to cool completely.

Dust liberally with icing sugar and cut into slices to serve. Store in an airtight container in a cool cupboard or the refrigerator and eat within 2 days.

pies, tarts & cheesecakes

classic apple pie

Apple pie afficionados believe that the best pies are made with a variety of apples to combine sweet and tart flavours with firm and melting textures. Serve this classic pie warm with vanilla ice cream or chilled cream.

1.3 kg mixed apples, such as Cox's, Braeburn and Golden Delicious, peeled and cored

50 g caster sugar, or more to taste

1 teaspoon ground cinnamon

1 tablespoon freshly squeezed lemon juice

vanilla ice cream or chilled single cream, to serve

American pie crust:

300 g plain flour

1 teaspoon caster sugar

¼ teaspoon salt

75 g unsalted butter

75 g lard or vegetable shortening

1 egg yolk

1 egg, beaten

caster sugar, for sprinkling

a pie dish or plate (with sloping sides), 23–25 cm diameter, greased

serves 6–8

To make the pastry, put the flour, sugar and salt in a food processor and process until just combined. Add the butter and lard and process using the pulse button until the mixture just forms coarse crumbs. Add the egg yolk and 4 tablespoons cold water and pulse again; the mixture should be crumbly and not holding together. Transfer to a floured work surface and form into a ball. Cut in half, wrap well in clingfilm and chill in the refrigerator for at least 1 hour (if leaving longer, double wrap as the dough dries out easily).

When ready to make the pie, roll out one dough half on a floured work surface and use it to line the bottom of the prepared pie dish. Trim the edges leaving a 1 cm overhang and save the pastry trimmings for decoration if liked. Chill while you prepare the apples.

Cut the apples into slices; not too thick and not too thin. Put them in a bowl with the sugar, cinnamon and lemon juice and use your hands to mix well. Transfer the apple mixture to the dough-lined pie dish.

Preheat the oven to 190°C (375°F) Gas 5.

Roll out the remaining dough on a floured work surface to a round large enough to cover the apples. Brush the edges of the dough in the dish with beaten egg, then lay the other pastry round on top. Fold over the overhang from the bottom layer and crimp together using your fingertips, or use the tines of a fork to seal. Decorate as desired (a few leaves are traditional) and brush lightly with egg, then sprinkle with sugar. Cut 6–8 small slits in the top of the pie.

Put on a baking tray and bake in the preheated oven for about 50–60 minutes, until golden. Serve warm with vanilla ice cream on the side or chilled single cream for pouring. Store any leftovers in an airtight container in the refrigerator and eat within 1 day.

key lime pie

You may well be apprehensive about using condensed milk in this recipe, but don't be; the sharp lime juice counters the intense sweetness, yielding a tangy but deeply satisfying creamy filling.

lime filling:

4 eggs, separated

400-g tin condensed milk

2 tablespoons finely grated lime zest

150 ml freshly squeezed lime juice (5–6 limes)

¼ teaspoon cream of tartar

cream topping:

250 ml whipping cream

3 tablespoons caster sugar

½ teaspoon vanilla extract

zest of 1 large lime, pared into fine shreds

sweet tart pastry:

180 g plain flour

a pinch of salt

40 g icing sugar

100 g unsalted butter, chilled and cut into cubes

1 large egg, separated

1½–2 tablespoons iced water

a loose-bottomed fluted tart tin, 23–25 cm diameter
baking beans

serves 6–8

To make the pastry, put the flour, salt, sugar and butter in a food processor fitted with a metal blade. Process until the mixture has a sandy appearance. Add the egg yolk and 1½ tablespoons of iced water and process again until the dough forms a ball and leaves the side of the bowl. Add extra water if the dough seems dry and crumbly. Form the dough into a ball, wrap in foil and chill in the refrigerator for 1 hour. Let the dough return to room temperature before rolling out.

Put the dough on a lightly floured work surface and roll it out fairly thinly. Use it to line the tart tin. Prick the base of the tart case all over with a fork and chill for 30–40 minutes.

Preheat the oven to 190°C (375°C) Gas 5. Line the tart case with foil or baking paper, fill with baking beans and bake blind in the preheated oven for 10–12 minutes. Remove the foil and baking beans and brush the inside of the pastry case with beaten egg white. Return to the oven for another 8–10 minutes, until the pastry is golden brown and crisp. Reduce the oven temperature to 180°C (350°F) Gas 4.

To make the lime filling, put 1 whole egg and 3 egg yolks in a bowl and beat until blended. Whisk in the condensed milk and lime zest. Gradually whisk in the lime juice. Put the egg whites and cream of tartar in a separate, grease-free bowl and whisk until stiff but not dry. Beat 2 tablespoons of the egg white mixture into the egg yolk mixture, then fold in the remainder with a spatula. Spoon into the pastry case and bake in the preheated oven for about 20 minutes, or until risen and just firm in the centre. Set the tin on a wire rack and leave to cool before unmoulding the pie.

To make the topping, put the cream, vanilla extract and 2 tablespoons of the sugar in a bowl. Whip until stiff, then spread over the cooled lime filling. Toss the shreds of lime zest in the remaining sugar and use to decorate. Serve cold but not chilled. Store any leftovers in an airtight container in the refrigerator and eat within 1 day.

lemon meringue pie

It's the cloud of fluffy, crisp-crusted meringue that makes this classic pie so appealing. You could use good-quality shop-bought lemon curd instead of making the filling here, but it is well worth the effort if you have the time.

1 recipe Sweet Tart Pastry
(see page 117)

lemon filling:

1 large egg and 3 large
egg yolks

125 g caster sugar

finely grated zest and freshly
squeezed juice of 2 large lemons

125 g unsalted butter, melted
and cooled

125 ml whipping cream

meringue topping:

3 large egg whites

¼ teaspoon cream of tartar

125 g caster sugar, plus
1 tablespoon to sprinkle

½ teaspoon finely grated
lemon zest

a loose-bottomed fluted tart tin,
20–23 cm diameter

serves 6–8

Preheat the oven to 190°C (375°F) Gas 5. Bring the pastry to room temperature, roll out and use it to line the tart tin. Bake blind following the method given on page 117. Reduce the oven temperature to 170°C (325°F) Gas 3.

To make the filling, put the egg, egg yolks and sugar in a bowl and beat together until slightly thickened and a paler yellow. Beat in the lemon zest, butter, cream and finally the lemon juice. Pour the filling into the pastry case and bake in the preheated oven for 20–30 minutes until the filling is barely set in the centre. Do not let it overbake.

To make the meringue, put the egg whites and cream of tartar in a grease-free bowl and, using an electric whisk, whisk until frothy and the whisk leaves stiff peaks. Whisk in half the sugar until the meringue is thick and glossy. Fold in the remaining sugar and the lemon zest using a metal spoon.

Pile the meringue onto the lemon filling, swirling and peaking as you go, covering the lemon filling completely. Sprinkle with the 1 tablespoon sugar and return the pie to the oven for another 30–35 minutes or until the meringue is browned and crisp on the outside. Serve just warm or cold. Store any leftovers in an airtight container in the refrigerator and eat within 2 days.

Baking Tip: When whisking egg whites, always use a clean, grease-free bowl. Plastic bowls are not recommended as the surface is difficult to clean completely; use a glass, ceramic, stainless-steel or copper bowl.

pumpkin pie

In America, this traditional festive pie is often made from tinned pumpkin or packaged pumpkin pie filling (spices included); it's a seasonal product available in bakeries and grocery stores. Home-made purée makes a delicious and wholesome substitute if tinned pumpkin is not available where you are.

1 recipe American Pie Crust
(see page 114)

pumpkin filling:

500 ml pumpkin purée*

100 g light soft brown sugar

3 large eggs

200 ml evaporated milk

120 ml golden syrup

a good pinch of salt

1 teaspoon ground cinnamon

½ teaspoon ground mixed spice

1 teaspoon vanilla extract

2 tablespoons dark rum

2 tart tins or pie plates,
22 cm diameter

makes two 22-cm pies

Preheat the oven to 190°C (375°F) Gas 5.

Roll out the pastry thinly on a lightly floured work surface, then use to line the tart tins. Trim and crimp or decorate the edges as you wish. Prick the bases all over with a fork, chill or freeze for 15 minutes, then bake blind following the method given on page 117. Reduce the oven temperature to 170°C (325°F) Gas 3.

Put all the filling ingredients in a food processor and process until smooth. Pour into the pastry cases, set on a baking tray and bake in the preheated oven for about 1 hour or until just set. Remove from the oven and leave to stand for 10 minutes, then carefully remove the pies from the tart tins and leave to cool for a few minutes. Serve warm or at room temperature, not chilled. Store any leftovers in an airtight container in the refrigerator and eat within 2 days.

* To make the purée, cut a pumpkin into large chunks. Place in a roasting tin and roast for about 1 hour at 170°C (325°F) Gas 3. Scrape the flesh from the skin and purée in a food processor until smooth. If the purée is fibrous, press it through a sieve to achieve a smooth texture.

mississippi mud pie

Not strictly speaking a pie, this famous dessert comes from the South of the USA – it is supposed to look like the thick, dark, muddy waters of the Mississippi delta. It is very easy to make and perfect for sharing.

biscuit base:

225 g digestives or other wheaten biscuits

60 g unsalted butter

60 g dark chocolate, chopped

chocolate filling:

180 g dark chocolate, chopped

180 g unsalted butter, cut into cubes

4 large eggs, beaten

90 g light muscovado sugar

90 g dark muscovado sugar

180 ml double cream

chocolate cream:

140 ml extra thick double cream, chilled

3 tablespoons cocoa powder

40 g icing sugar

a springform cake tin, 23 cm diameter, well buttered

serves 8

To make the base, put the biscuits into a food processor and process until fine crumbs form. Alternatively, put the biscuits into a plastic bag and crush with a rolling pin. Transfer the crumbs to a mixing bowl.

Put the butter and chocolate in a heatproof bowl set over a saucepan of simmering but not boiling water and melt gently (do not let the base of the bowl touch the water). Remove from the heat, stir gently, then stir into the biscuit crumbs. When well mixed, transfer the mixture to the prepared tin and, using the back of a spoon, press onto the base and about halfway up the sides of the tin. Chill while making the filling.

Preheat the oven to 180°C (350°F) Gas 4. To make the filling, put the chocolate and butter in a heatproof bowl set over a saucepan of simmering but not boiling water and melt gently (do not let the base of the bowl touch the water). Remove from the heat, stir gently and set aside to cool.

Put the eggs and sugar into a mixing bowl and, using an electric whisk or mixer, whisk until thick and foamy. Whisk in the cream followed by the melted chocolate. Pour the mixture into the biscuit case and bake in the preheated oven for about 45 minutes until just firm. Leave to cool for a few minutes, then remove from the tin.

To make the chocolate cream, put the cream into a mixing bowl, then sift the cocoa and icing sugar on top and stir gently with a wooden spoon until blended. Cover and chill.

Serve the pie at room temperature with the chocolate cream on the side. Remove from the refrigerator about 30 minutes before serving. Store any leftovers in an airtight container in the refrigerator and eat within 2 days.

double chocolate brownie tart with walnut crust

This ingenious tart has a classic brownie filling baked within a deliciously nutty biscuit case. Best served warm from the oven (or wrapped in foil and gently reheated in a low oven) with a scoop of vanilla ice cream on the side.

150 g digestives or other wheaten biscuits

150 g walnuts

125 g unsalted butter, melted

brownie filling:

125 g dark chocolate, broken into small pieces

175 g unsalted butter, softened

400 g caster sugar

3 large eggs, beaten

1 teaspoon vanilla extract

150 g plain flour

200 g white chocolate chips

a deep cake tin, 23 cm square, base-lined with baking paper

makes about 16 pieces

To make the base, crush the biscuits and walnuts together in a food processor, pulsing to keep the biscuits and nuts quite coarse. Stir the biscuits into the melted butter until evenly coated. Press evenly into the base and 4 cm up the sides of the prepared tin before it cools. Chill in the refrigerator for 20 minutes to set the case before filling.

Preheat the oven to 180°C (350°F) Gas 4.

To make the filling, put the chocolate in a heatproof bowl set over a saucepan of simmering but not boiling water and melt gently (do not let the base of the bowl touch the water). Put the butter and sugar into another bowl, cream together until light and fluffy, then beat in the eggs. Stir in the melted chocolate and vanilla extract. Fold in the flour, then half the chocolate chips. Spoon into the biscuit case and level the surface. Sprinkle with the remaining chocolate chips.

Bake in the preheated oven for 35 minutes, or until a cocktail stick inserted into the centre reveals fudgy crumbs. Do not overcook as this will make the brownie filling too dry. Leave to cool in the tin.

When completely cool, turn out of the tin, peel off the lining paper and cut the tart into 16 squares. Store any leftovers in an airtight container in a cool cupboard or the refrigerator and eat within 4 days.

cranberry and cinnamon crunch tart

A delightful cross between a biscuit and a cake – this light streusel pastry has a texture much like shortbread, and is filled with a layer of thick cranberry sauce, providing a sharp contrast to its butteriness. Delicious cut into wedges and served with coffee.

streusel pastry:

250 g unsalted butter, softened

50 g caster sugar

2 tablespoons sunflower oil

1 teaspoon vanilla extract

1 egg, beaten

450 g plain flour

1 teaspoon baking powder

¼ teaspoon salt

2 teaspoons ground cinnamon

cranberry sauce:

350 g fresh or frozen cranberries

125 g caster sugar

finely grated zest and freshly squeezed juice of 1 orange

to finish:

75 g demerara sugar

icing sugar, to dust

a springform cake tin, 25 cm diameter, base-lined with baking paper and buttered and floured

serves 12

To make the cranberry sauce, put the cranberries and sugar into a food processor and chop coarsely. Transfer to a saucepan and add the orange zest and juice. Bring to the boil, stirring constantly. Simmer for 5 minutes, then set aside to cool completely.

To make the streusel pastry, cream the butter and sugar together in a bowl until light and fluffy. Beat in the sunflower oil and vanilla extract, then beat in the egg. Sift the flour, baking powder, salt and cinnamon together into a separate bowl. Gradually stir the wet ingredients into the dry, until the dough resembles a coarse shortbread mixture. Bring the dough together with your hands and knead lightly into a ball. Wrap and chill for at least 2 hours or until very firm. When the dough is thoroughly chilled, remove from the refrigerator and divide into 2 pieces. Immediately re-wrap and return the piece you are not using to the refrigerator.

Preheat the oven to 150°C (300°F) Gas 2.

Grate the first piece of dough coarsely into the prepared tin to cover the base evenly. Do not pack down. Carefully spoon in the cold cranberry sauce, avoiding the edges. Remove the remaining dough from the refrigerator and grate evenly over the top, then sprinkle liberally with demerara sugar to finish. Bake in the preheated oven for about 1¼–1½ hours, until pale but firm.

Leave to cool in the tin, then unclip and carefully remove the tart from the tin. Dust with icing sugar to serve. Store any leftovers in an airtight container in a cool cupboard or the refrigerator and eat within 6 days.

simple lemon cheese tart

The technique used here of blending the sugar with large peelings of lemon zest, transfers all the essential oils to the sugar and gives a wonderful aroma to the tart. For a lighter result, and to cut a few calories, you can replace the cream cheese with cottage cheese.

1 recipe Sweet Tart Pastry
(see page 117)

1 lemon

75 g caster sugar

350 g full-fat cream cheese

1 egg, plus 3 egg yolks

2 teaspoons vanilla extract

a loose-bottomed fluted tart tin,
23 cm diameter

serves 4–6

Preheat the oven to 190°C (375°F) Gas 5.

Bring the pastry to room temperature. Roll out the pastry on a lightly floured work surface and use it to line the tart tin. Prick the base, then chill or freeze for 15 minutes. Bake blind following the method given on page 117. Leave to cool.

Peel the zest from the lemon leaving behind any white pith, and squeeze the juice. Put the lemon zest and sugar into a food processor and process until mixture looks damp.

Add the lemon juice and process again – the lemon zest should be completely dissolved into the sugar. Add the cream cheese, whole egg, egg yolks and vanilla extract. Process until smooth and pour the mixture into the pastry case.

Bake in the preheated oven for about 25 minutes, until just set and lightly browned on top. Leave to cool. Serve at room temperature. Store any leftovers in an airtight container in the refrigerator and eat within 2 days.

pear, almond and mascarpone tart

This recipe works best if the pears are on the overripe side so that they are fork-tender when cooked. The addition of creamy mascarpone cheese gives this tart an irresistible melt-in-the-mouth texture.

4 very ripe pears

1 tablespoon freshly squeezed lemon juice

4 tablespoons caster sugar

125 g mascarpone cheese

1 egg

1 tablespoon plain flour

100 g flaked almonds

2 tablespoons granulated sugar

chilled single cream, to serve

push-it-in pastry:

200 g plain flour

4 tablespoons caster sugar

80 g unsalted butter, chilled and cut into cubes

a loose-bottomed fluted tart tin, 24 cm diameter, lightly greased and floured

serves 8–10

To make the pastry, put the flour and sugar in a food processor and pulse to combine. With the motor running, add the butter and 1–2 tablespoons cold water and mix until the mixture resembles coarse breadcrumbs and starts to gather in lumps. Transfer to a lightly floured work surface and briefly knead to form a ball. Wrap in clingfilm and chill in the refrigerator for 1 hour, until firm.

Preheat the oven to 180°C (350°F) Gas 4.

Coarsely grate the chilled pastry into a large bowl. Using lightly floured hands, scatter the grated pastry into the prepared tart tin and use your fingers to gently press it in until the entire base and the side of the tin are covered. Bake in the preheated oven for about 25 minutes, until lightly golden. Leave to cool.

Peel, halve and core the pears. Put them in a non-reactive bowl with the lemon juice and 1 tablespoon of the caster sugar. Put the remaining caster sugar in a food processor. Add the mascarpone, egg and flour and process to form a thick paste. Spread the mixture over the pastry. Arrange the pears on top and scatter with the almonds and granulated sugar. Bake in the oven for 40–45 minutes, until the pears are soft and the mascarpone mixture has set. Serve warm or at room temperature with chilled single cream for pouring. Store any leftovers in an airtight container in the refrigerator and eat within 1 day.

free-form caramelized peach tart

Ready-made puff pastry makes light work of preparing this fresh fruit tart – if you can buy it ready-rolled there is even less effort required! Use soft, ripe peaches here for the best result. Plums makes a good alternative.

500 g ready-made puff pastry, defrosted if frozen

4–6 ripe peaches

55 g unsalted butter

freshly squeezed juice of ½ a lemon

150 g caster sugar

crème fraîche, to serve

a dinner plate, 28 cm diameter (to use as a template)

serves 6

Preheat the oven to 230°C (450°F) Gas 8.

Roll out the pastry on a lightly floured work surface and cut out a round, 28 cm diameter, using a large dinner plate as a template. Lift onto a baking tray and make an edge by twisting the pastry over itself all the way around the edge. Press lightly to seal. Still on the baking tray, chill or freeze for at least 15 minutes.

Peel the peaches if necessary, then halve and stone them and cut into chunky slices. Put the butter into a saucepan, then add the lemon juice and half the sugar. Heat until melted, then add the peaches and toss gently.

Arrange the peaches all over the pastry. Sprinkle with the remaining sugar and bake in the preheated oven for 20–25 minutes until golden, puffed and caramelized. Serve with crème fraîche. This tart is best eaten on the day it is made.

white chocolate and raspberry tartlets

These indulgent little fresh fruit tarts look elegant and taste really good, yet they are very simple to make. When buying ready-made puff pastry, look for brands which say they are 'all-butter' as these will have the best flavour.

300 g ready-made puff pastry, defrosted if frozen

100 g good-quality white chocolate, broken into pieces

2 eggs

100 ml double cream

50 g caster sugar

about 300 g fresh raspberries

icing sugar, to dust

a 12-hole muffin tin

a pastry cutter roughly the same size as the muffin tin holes

makes 12 small tartlets

Preheat the oven to 180°C (350°F) Gas 4.

Roll out the pastry on a lightly floured work surface to a thickness of 2 mm. Cut the dough into rounds using the pastry cutter and press these gently into the muffin tin holes.

Put the chocolate in a heatproof bowl set over a saucepan of simmering but not boiling water and melt gently (do not let the base of the bowl touch the water). Stir the chocolate with a wooden spoon until it has melted. Remove from the heat and leave to cool slightly.

Put the eggs in a large bowl and beat with a balloon whisk until smooth. Whisk in the cream and sugar. Whisk in the melted chocolate until the mixture is smooth.

Carefully fill the pastry cases with the white chocolate mixture using a small spoon. Bake in the preheated oven for about 15 minutes, until the pastry is puffy and golden and the filling is risen (it will fall as the tartlets cool). Leave the tartlets to cool in the tin, then carefully turn them out. Arrange 3 raspberries on top of each tartlet and dust with icing sugar. These tartlets are best eaten on the day they are made. Keep covered and refrigerated until ready to serve.

Baking Tip: Stack trimmings of puff or flaky pastry on top of each other, rather than pressing them into a ball, before rolling them again. This will help to keep the all-important layers intact.

fresh raspberry tart

This impressive tart is simplicity itself to make, but must be assembled at the last moment to keep the freshness and crispness of the pastry. You may like to brush the inside of the cooled tart case with melted white chocolate before filling it. This will help to keep the pastry crisp, and make the tart even more of an indulgent treat!

1 recipe Sweet Tart Pastry (see page 117)

2–3 tablespoons raspberry jam

600 ml double cream, or 300 ml double cream mixed with 300 ml crème fraîche

2 tablespoons framboise liqueur, (optional)

750 g fresh raspberries

150 ml raspberry or redcurrant jelly (or any berry jelly will do)

a loose-bottomed fluted tart tin, 20.5 cm diameter

serves 6–8

Preheat the oven to 200°C (400°F) Gas 6 and bring the pastry to room temperature. Roll out the pastry thinly on a lightly floured work surface, and use it to line the tart tin. Prick the base all over, chill or freeze for 15 minutes, then bake blind following the method given on page 117. Leave to cool.

Press the raspberry jam through a sieve to remove the seeds, then put it into a large bowl. Add the cream and framboise liqueur, if using. Whisk until thick and just holding peaks. Spoon into the tart case and level the surface. Cover with the raspberries, arranging a final neat layer on top.

Put the raspberry or redcurrant jelly into a small saucepan and warm it gently until liquid. Brush over the raspberries to glaze. Put into the refrigerator to chill and set for 10 minutes only before serving (no longer or the tart will go soggy).

*Note: If liked, you could decorate the top of the tart with white chocolate curls (use a chocolate with a low cocoa solids content, bring it to room temperature first, then shave with a potato peeler).

little richmond maids of honour tartlets

These were named after the ladies (maids of honour) who carried them back to Richmond Palace for King Henry VIII or Queen Elizabeth I – both monarchs, it is said, loved these little cheesecakes made by a local baker. Make them in small, deep tins (like mini-brioche tins) if you can find them, as the filling seems to stay more moist and they look great!

1 recipe Sweet Tart Pastry
(see page 117)

filling:

50 g unsalted butter

75 g caster sugar

finely grated zest and juice
of 1 lemon

125 g curd or cottage cheese

2 large eggs, beaten

75 ml brandy or cherry brandy

125 g ground almonds

a pinch of salt

12 tablespoons cherry conserve

8 small sprigs of fresh rosemary
(optional)

icing sugar, for dusting

8 small loose-bottomed tartlet
tins, 10 cm diameter

a pastry cutter, about 12–14 cm
diameter

makes 8 tartlets

Bring the pastry to room temperature. Roll it out thinly on a lightly floured work surface and use the pastry cutter to stamp out small rounds, slightly larger than the tartlet tins. Carefully ease each pastry round into a tin. Prick the bases with a fork. Stand on a baking tray and chill for 30 minutes.

Preheat the oven to 180°C (350°F) Gas 4.

Put the butter, sugar and lemon zest in a large bowl and, using a wooden spoon or electric hand mixer, beat together until pale and fluffy. Strain the curd or cottage cheese into another bowl (do not blend in a food processor, otherwise the texture will be altered), then beat the cheese into the butter and sugar mixture. Beat in the eggs, lemon juice and brandy, then gently fold in the ground almonds and salt.

Drop a teaspoon of cherry conserve in each pastry case, then add the almond filling to about two-thirds full to leave room for rising. Bake in the preheated oven for 20–25 minutes, until risen and golden brown. Leave to cool slightly in the tartlet tins before carefully turning out. Spear each cheesecake with a small sprig of fresh rosemary, if using, and dust with icing sugar. Serve warm or at room temperature. These tartlets are best eaten on the day they are made. Keep covered until ready to serve.

classic baked cheesecake

A good baked cheesecake is everyone's favourite. Make this the day before you plan to serve it for a good flavour. For the best result, bring the cream cheese, eggs and soured cream to room temperature before using.

160 g very dry, slightly sweet biscuits, such as rich tea

225 g caster sugar

100 g unsalted butter, melted

750 g full-fat cream cheese

5 eggs

1 teaspoon finely grated lemon zest

300 ml soured cream

a springform cake tin, 23 cm diameter, lined with baking paper and lightly greased

serves 8–10

Preheat the oven to 170°C (325°F) Gas 3. Wrap the entire outside of the prepared cake tin in a double layer of foil.

Put the biscuits and 1 tablespoon of the sugar in a food processor and process to a fine crumb. Add the melted butter and process until well combined. Tip the crumb mixture into the prepared tin and spread evenly over the base. Firmly press the crumb mixture into the tin. Bake in the preheated oven for 20 minutes. Remove and leave to cool completely.

Put the cream cheese and remaining sugar in a mixing bowl, preferably that of a free-standing electric mixer with a paddle attachment, and beat together for 2 minutes, until smooth and well combined. Add the eggs, 1 at a time, beating well between each addition and scraping down the side of the bowl. Add the lemon zest and soured cream. Beat until smooth.

Pour the mixture into the prepared tin and level the surface. Bake in the oven for about 1 hour, until the top is golden but the centre still wobbly. Turn the oven off and partially open the oven door. Leave the cheesecake to cool in the oven for 1 hour then refrigerate for at least 6 hours, ideally overnight.

Remove the cheesecake from the refrigerator 1 hour before serving. Run a warm, round-bladed knife around the edge, then unclip and carefully remove the tin. Cut into generous wedges to serve. This cheesecake is best eaten the day after making. Keep covered and refrigerated until ready to serve.

> *Baking Tip: For many baking recipes – including cheesecakes, pastries and meringues – eggs should be brought to room temperature for the best results. Take them out of the fridge 30–60 minutes before using.*

lemon and ginger cheesecake

The water-bath method for baking cheesecakes is the best way of producing a silky smooth, velvety-textured filling that melts on the tongue. This is a delicate cheesecake that's best chilled overnight in its baking tin and unmoulded the following day.

225 g digestives or other wheaten biscuits

2 tablespoons caster sugar

2 teaspoons ground ginger

125 g unsalted butter, melted

cheesecake filling:

570 g full-fat cream cheese or curd cheese

180 g caster sugar

1 tablespoon cornflour

4 large eggs, beaten

finely grated zest of 2 lemons

380 ml soured cream

ginger topping:

250 ml sour cream

2½ tablespoons caster sugar

80 g stem ginger in syrup, drained and finely chopped

finely grated zest of 1 lemon

a springform cake tin, 25 cm diameter, lined with baking paper

a roasting tin, big enough to comfortably take the cake tin

serves 8–10

Preheat the oven to 180°C (350°F) Gas 4.

Wrap the entire outside of the prepared cake tin in a double layer of foil, moulding it to the tin, but being very careful not to puncture it so that it remains completely watertight.

Put the biscuits in a food processor and pulse to form fine crumbs. Add the sugar and ground ginger and blend again. Transfer to a bowl and stir in the melted butter until evenly mixed. Spoon the crumb mixture into the prepared tin and, using the back of a spoon, press down to form an even layer over the base and up the side of the tin. Bake in the preheated oven for 10–12 minutes to set the crust, then leave to cool. Do not turn off the oven.

To make the filling, put the cream cheese and sugar in a large bowl and beat together until smooth. Beat in the cornflour, followed by the eggs in about 4 portions. When smooth, beat in the lemon zest and sour cream. Pour the mixture over the crumb base. Set the cake tin in the roasting tin and pour very hot water into the roasting tin to come just over halfway up the sides of the cake tin. Transfer the tins to the oven and bake for 45–50 minutes, until just set in the centre.

Meanwhile, to make the ginger topping, put the soured cream and 2 tablespoons of the sugar in a bowl and mix well. Take the cheesecake out of the oven and carefully spread the sour cream mixture over the surface. Sprinkle the chopped ginger evenly over the whole surface, then return to the oven for 10 minutes. Remove the cheesecake from its water bath, leave it to cool on a wire rack, then chill, ideally overnight, before removing the foil and unmoulding the cheesecake. Toss the grated lemon zest with the remaining sugar and use to decorate the cheesecake just before serving. This cheesecake is best eaten the day after making. Keep covered and refrigerated until ready to serve.

warm chocolate cheesecake

This slightly unusual cheesecake is based on an Italian recipe. It is very light in texture yet full of flavour and can be eaten warm or at room temperature with a dollop of thick cream on the side.

biscuit base:

225 g digestives or other wheaten biscuits

60 g unsalted butter

60 g dark chocolate, finely chopped

chocolate filling:

2 large eggs, separated

85 g caster sugar

230 g mascarpone cheese

150 ml double cream, lightly whipped

50 g dark chocolate, very finely chopped

4 tablespoons cocoa powder

45 g ground almonds

1–2 tablespoons Amaretto liqueur or brandy

icing sugar, for dusting

thick cream, to serve

a springform cake tin, 23 cm diameter, well buttered

serves 8

To make the base, put the biscuits in a food processor and pulse until fine crumbs form. Alternatively, put the biscuits into a plastic bag and crush with a rolling pin. Transfer the crumbs to a mixing bowl. Put the butter and chocolate in a heatproof bowl set over a saucepan of simmering but not boiling water and melt gently (do not let the base of the bowl touch the water). Remove from the heat, stir gently, then stir into the biscuit crumbs. When well mixed, transfer the mixture to the prepared tin and, using the back of a spoon, press onto the base and about halfway up the sides of the tin. Chill while making the filling.

Preheat the oven to 170°C (325°F) Gas 3. To make the filling, put the egg yolks and sugar into a large mixing bowl and, using an electric whisk or mixer, whisk until very thick and mousse-like – when the whisk is lifted, a wide ribbon-like trail should slowly fall back into the bowl. Put the mascarpone into a separate bowl, beat until smooth, then gently fold in the whipped cream. Gently stir the mascarpone mixture into the egg yolks, then add the chopped chocolate, sifted cocoa, ground almonds and liqueur and mix gently.

Put the egg whites in a separate spotlessly clean, grease-free bowl and, using an electric whisk or mixer, whisk until stiff peaks form. Using a large metal spoon, fold the egg whites into the chocolate mixture in 3 batches.

Pour the filling into the biscuit case and bake in the preheated oven for about 1 hour, or until set and beginning to colour. Leave to cool for about 20 minutes, then carefully unclip and remove the tin.

Dust with icing sugar and serve warm or at room temperature with a dollop of thick cream on the side. This cheesecake is best eaten still warm, on the day of making. Keep covered until ready to serve.

ricotta and muscatel raisin baked cheesecake

This rich cheesecake is perfect for a special occasion and the pastry contains pine nuts which add a delicious flavour and texture. The surface of most cheesecakes will split when baking so don't worry – it adds character!

pastry:

225 g fine polenta

75 g plain flour

125 g caster sugar

55 g toasted pine nuts

175 g unsalted butter, cut into cubes

2 large egg yolks

filling:

75 g large Muscatel raisins, soaked in 2–3 tablespoons Vin Santo or Marsala wine for several hours

500 g ricotta

500 g full-fat cream cheese

240 ml soured cream

4 large eggs, separated

125 g caster sugar

2 teaspoons vanilla extract

a pinch of salt

freshly grated nutmeg, to taste

a springform cake tin, 23 cm diameter, greased and base-lined with baking paper

baking beans

serves 8–10

To make the pastry, put the polenta, flour, sugar, pine nuts and butter in a food processor and process, in short bursts, until the mixture resembles coarse breadcrumbs. Add the egg yolks and process until the dough forms a ball. Wrap in clingfilm and chill in the refrigerator for 1 hour.

Preheat the oven to 180°C (350°F) Gas 4.

Roll out the pastry on a sheet of lightly floured, greaseproof paper to about 7 mm thickness and carefully use to line the cake tin. Chill for 5 minutes. Cut out a large piece of baking paper to fit the tin, put it on top of the pastry case, then fill with baking beans.

Bake in the preheated oven for 10 minutes. Remove the baking paper and beans and return to the oven for a further 10 minutes. Leave to cool. Do not turn off the oven.

Put the ricotta, cream cheese and soured cream in a large bowl and, using a wooden spoon or electric hand mixer, beat well. Put the egg yolks and sugar in a separate bowl and beat together until light and creamy. Add the cheese mixture and vanilla extract and beat until smooth. Fold in the raisins.

Put the egg whites and salt in a separate, spotlessly clean, grease-free bowl. Using a balloon whisk or electric mixer, whisk until soft peaks form, then fold into the cheese mixture. Spoon the filling into the pastry case and sprinkle grated nutmeg generously over the top.

Bake in the preheated oven for 30–40 minutes, until golden but still a little soft in the centre. Leave to cool for about 20 minutes, then carefully unclip and remove the tin. This cheesecake is best eaten at room temperature on the day of making. Keep covered until ready to serve.

breads, buns & scones

buttermilk cornbread

Stoneground yellow cornmeal gives this cornbread a wonderful texture, and the buttermilk and honey make for a soft, sweet crumb. For a change, you could add 3 tablespoons of toasted pine nuts, fresh or frozen sweetcorn kernels, or grated mature Cheddar cheese.

140 g fine yellow cornmeal, preferably stoneground

125 g plain flour

1½ teaspoons baking powder

½ teaspoon bicarbonate of soda

½ teaspoon salt

1 large egg

4 tablespoons melted butter

3 tablespoons clear honey

225 ml buttermilk

a cake tin, 20 cm square, well greased

serves 6–8

Preheat the oven to 200°C (400°F) Gas 6.

Put the cornmeal, flour, baking powder, bicarbonate of soda and salt in a large bowl and stir with a wooden spoon until thoroughly mixed.

In a separate bowl, beat the egg with the melted butter, honey and buttermilk. Stir into the dry ingredients to make a thick, smooth batter. Transfer the mixture to the prepared tin and level the surface.

Bake in the preheated oven for 15–20 minutes until golden and a skewer inserted in the centre comes out clean. Turn out onto a board, cut into large squares, and serve warm.

This cornbread is best eaten warm on the day of making but it can be frozen for up to 1 month.

fluffy American biscuits

Eaten hot, split and spread with butter and jam, these 'dropped' American biscuits are popular in the southern states. For a light crumb, handle the dough as little as possible, barely enough to combine the ingredients. For savoury biscuits to eat with thick soups and stews, add 50 g chopped ham or crumbled cooked bacon to the mixture before adding the buttermilk.

250 g plain flour, plus extra for dusting

1 tablespoon baking powder

½ teaspoon bicarbonate of soda

½ teaspoon salt

2 teaspoons caster sugar

40 g unsalted butter, chilled and cut into cubes

about 300 ml buttermilk

melted butter, for brushing

a baking tray, lightly greased

makes 12 biscuits

Preheat the oven to 230°C (450°F) Gas 8.

Sift the flour, baking powder, bicarbonate of soda, salt and sugar into a large bowl.

Add the chilled butter and rub it in with the tips of your fingers until the mixture looks like fine crumbs. Make a well in the centre and pour in the buttermilk. Using a round-bladed knife, quickly and briefly stir the ingredients together to make a really rough-looking, damp dough that will fall off a spoon.

Take 1 heaped tablespoon of the dough and drop it onto the prepared baking tray to make a rough mound. Repeat with the rest of the dough, spacing the mounds about 2.5 cm apart – they will spread in the oven so the sides will touch.

Dust lightly with flour, then brush with melted butter and bake in the preheated oven for 12–15 minutes, until golden and firm to the touch. Transfer carefully to a wire rack and leave until cool enough to handle, then split and serve warm.

These biscuits are best eaten on the day of making or gently reheated the next day. They can be frozen for up to 1 month.

Baker's Tip: To test the freshness of baking powder, mix 2 teaspoons with 200 ml hot tap water. If there is an immediate fizzing and foaming action, the baking powder can be used. If there is little or no reaction or a delayed reaction, discard the baking powder.

apricot and honey rye bread

This unusual fruited bread is packed with dried apricots and is delicious lightly buttered and topped with honey, preserves or cheese.

100 g dried apricots, halved

2 tablespoons clear honey

140 ml very hot water

400 g strong white bread flour, sifted

100 g rye flour, plus extra for dusting

2 teaspoons salt

15 g fresh yeast*

140 ml whole milk, at room temperature

2 tablespoons melted butter

100 g whole blanched hazelnuts, toasted and halved

a 1-kg loaf tin, greased

makes 1 large loaf

Put the apricots in a heatproof bowl with the honey and pour over the very hot water. Stir well, then leave, uncovered, until the water is tepid and the honey has dissolved.

Mix the flours in a large bowl and add the salt. Make a well in the centre. Crumble the fresh yeast into a small jug and whisk in the milk until blended. Pour into the well with the melted butter, then add the apricots and their soaking liquid. Mix in the flour to make a soft but not sticky dough. If the dough is too dry or too sticky, add extra water or flour, 1 tablespoon at a time.

Work in the nuts, then turn the dough out onto a lightly floured surface and knead thoroughly for 10 minutes. Put in an oiled bowl and cover with a damp tea towel or put the bowl in an oiled plastic bag. Leave to rise at room temperature until doubled in size – about 1½ hours. Punch down the risen dough with your knuckles, then turn it out onto a surface dusted with rye flour. Shape into a loaf and press gently into the prepared tin. Cover and leave to rise as before at room temperature until doubled in size – about 1 hour. Meanwhile, preheat the oven to 220°C (425°F) Gas 7.

Bake the uncovered loaf in the preheated oven for 35–40 minutes until golden brown and sounds hollow when turned out and tapped underneath. Leave to cool on a wire rack. This loaf is best eaten within 4 days. When thoroughly cooled, it can be wrapped then frozen for up to 1 month.

* To use easy-blend dried yeast, mix one 7 g sachet with the flours and salt. Add the milk, melted butter and apricot mixture, then proceed with the recipe.

maple pecan loaf

This loaf combines two favourite American ingredients to make a bread rich in flavour, but not too sweet. Using wholemeal flour and roasting the pecans enhances the nuttiness. It makes a good breakfast bread, or works well with ham or cheese for sandwiches.

350 g strong stoneground wholemeal bread flour

350 g unbleached strong white bread flour

2 teaspoons salt

200 g pecans, lightly toasted and coarsely chopped

15 g fresh yeast*

375 ml tepid water

150 g maple syrup

two 450-g loaf tins, lightly greased

makes 2 medium loaves

Mix the flours, salt and nuts in a large mixing bowl and make a well in the centre. Crumble the yeast into a small bowl, pour in half the water, then stir until thoroughly blended. Pour into the well, followed by the rest of the water and the maple syrup. Mix the ingredients in the well, then gradually work in the flour to make a soft but not sticky dough. If the dough sticks to your fingers, work in extra flour, 1 tablespoon at a time; if the dough feels stiff and dry or there are crumbs in the base of the bowl, work in a little more water, 1 tablespoon at a time.

Turn the dough out onto a lightly floured work surface and knead thoroughly for 10 minutes until very elastic. Return the dough to the bowl, cover with clingfilm and leave to rise in a warm place until doubled in size, about 1½ hours.

Turn the risen dough out onto a lightly floured work surface and punch down to deflate. Divide the dough into 2 equal pieces and shape each into a loaf to fit the tins. Set a loaf into each prepared tin, then slip the tins into a large, oiled plastic bag, slightly inflated, close, then leave to rise as before until doubled in size, about 45–60 minutes. Meanwhile, preheat the oven to 200°C (400°F) Gas 6.

Bake the uncovered loaves in the preheated oven for about 30–35 minutes, until they are a good golden brown colour and sound hollow when turned out and tapped underneath. Leave to cool on a wire rack. This loaf is best eaten within 4 days. When thoroughly cooled, it can be wrapped then frozen for up to 1 month.

* To use easy-blend dried yeast, mix one 7 g sachet with the flours, salt and nuts. Add the water and syrup to the bowl and proceed with the recipe.

treacle soda bread

Black treacle adds a lovely depth of flavour to this Irish-style soda bread, which is excellent with butter and marmalade or sliced cheese. It is best made with stoneground wholemeal flour with a very coarse texture.

350 g coarse stoneground plain wholemeal flour

115 g plain white flour

1 teaspoon bicarbonate of soda

1 teaspoon salt

3 tablespoons sesame seeds

1 teaspoon light muscovado sugar

1 teaspoon ground ginger

25 g unsalted butter, chilled and cut into cubes

1 large egg

300 ml natural yoghurt

1½ tablespoons black treacle

a 450-g loaf tin, well greased

makes 1 medium loaf

Preheat the oven to 200°C (400°F) Gas 6.

Put the flours and bicarbonate of soda in a large bowl, then stir in the salt, 2 tablespoons of the sesame seeds, sugar and ginger. Mix well. Rub in the chilled butter using your fingertips until the mixture looks like fine crumbs.

Lightly beat the egg with the yoghurt and treacle in a separate bowl, then quickly stir into the dry mixture using a wooden spoon. With floured hands, knead the dough 2–3 times in the bowl so it just comes together. It should be heavy and sticky – quite unlike a scone dough or a yeasted bread dough. If it is too dry or too wet, add extra yoghurt or flour, 1 tablespoon at a time. (The exact amount of liquid needed will depend on the quality of the flour.) Shape the dough into a loaf to fit the tin, then gently roll it in the remaining sesame seeds to cover. Press the dough neatly into the prepared tin.

Bake in the preheated oven for 10 minutes, then reduce the oven temperature to 180°C (350°F) Gas 4 and bake for a further 35 minutes. (If it browns too quickly or too much, cover with foil or baking paper.) The cooked bread should be browned, well-risen and sound hollow when turned out and tapped underneath. If it sounds heavy or the crust is flabby, return the turned-out loaf to the oven for about 5 minutes, then test again.

Cool on a wire rack. Although this loaf is good the day it is baked, it tastes even better if wrapped and kept for a day before eating. When thoroughly cooled, the loaf can be wrapped then frozen for up to 1 month.

toasted teacakes

Squidgy in texture, and dripping with melted butter, nothing quite makes a tea time like hot buttered teacakes. These ones are small, rather than the traditional large ones, so there'll be plenty of room for those other tea-time cakes and fancies.

225 g strong white bread flour

½ teaspoon salt

1 teaspoon easy-blend dried yeast

1½ tablespoons light soft brown sugar

¼ teaspoon freshly grated nutmeg

50 g mixed dried fruit

3 dried apricots, chopped

40 g unsalted butter

120 ml whole milk, plus extra for brushing

butter, to serve

2 baking trays, greased

makes 8 small teacakes

Combine the flour, salt, yeast, sugar and nutmeg in a bowl, then sift into a larger bowl. Stir in the dried fruit and apricots and make a well in the centre of the mixture.

Melt the butter in a small saucepan, then add the milk and heat until lukewarm. Pour into the flour mixture, gradually working it in to make a soft dough. Turn out onto a lightly floured surface and knead for about 5 minutes until smooth and elastic. Transfer to a bowl, wrap in an oiled plastic bag and leave to rise in a warm place for about 1 hour until doubled in size.

Turn the dough out onto a lightly floured work surface, punch down and divide into 8 equal pieces. Shape each one into a ball, flatten slightly and arrange on the prepared baking trays, spacing them slightly apart. Wrap the baking trays in plastic bags and let rise in a warm place for about 45 minutes until doubled in size.

Meanwhile, preheat the oven to 200°C (400°F) Gas 6.

Brush the tops of the teacakes with milk, then bake in the preheated oven for about 15 minutes, until risen and golden and they sound hollow when tapped underneath. Transfer to a wire rack to cool. To serve, cut the teacakes in half and toast, then spread generously with butter. Store in an airtight container in a cool cupboard and eat within 2 days.

baby chelsea buns

These fruity, spiced, spiralled buns have been a traditional English treat since the 18th century. They were first made and sold by the celebrated Chelsea Bun House in Chelsea, west London. Sweet and sticky, and a mini version of the original, these are delicious served warm from the oven.

450 g strong white bread flour

1 teaspoon salt

50 g caster sugar

7-g sachet easy-blend dried yeast

90 g butter, melted

150 ml whole milk

2 eggs, beaten

80 g light soft brown sugar

1 teaspoon ground cinnamon

75 g sultanas

25 g currants

50 g dried apricots, chopped

clear honey, for brushing

a cake tin, 20 cm square, greased

makes 16 small buns

Combine the sifted flour, salt, caster sugar and yeast in a large bowl and make a well in the centre of the mixture. Put two thirds of the melted butter in a small saucepan with the milk and heat until lukewarm. Remove from the heat, stir in the beaten eggs, then pour into the flour mixture, gradually working it in to make a soft dough. Turn the dough out onto a lightly floured surface and knead for 5–10 minutes, until smooth and elastic. Return to the bowl, wrap in an oiled plastic bag and leave to rise in a warm place for about 1 hour, until doubled in size.

Punch down the dough, then divide into 4 equal pieces. Roll out each piece on a lightly floured surface to about 12 x 20 cm. Combine the brown sugar, cinnamon and dried fruits in a bowl and toss to mix. Pour the remaining melted butter over the dough, brushing it towards the edges to cover evenly. Sprinkle the fruit mixture on top and roll up tightly from the long edge to make 4 rolls. Slice each roll into 4 whirls and arrange them, cut-side up in the prepared cake tin so that they are barely touching. Wrap the tin in an oiled plastic bag and leave to rise in a warm place for about 30 minutes, until doubled in size. Meanwhile, preheat the oven to 200°C (400°F) Gas 6.

Take the cake tin out of the plastic bag and bake the buns in the preheated oven for about 20 minutes until golden. Brush with honey and bake for another 5 minutes. Leave to cool in the tin for about 10 minutes, then turn out onto a wire rack and leave to cool completely. Pull the buns apart to serve. When cool, store in an airtight container in a cool cupboard and eat within 3 days.

cider-apple doughnuts

This quick recipe for delicious American-style doughnuts is based on a rich potato-scone dough, introduced to New England by Irish farmers. It makes excellent, light and well-flavoured doughnuts.

2 medium-tart eating apples

1 teaspoon ground cinnamon

450 g plain white flour

¼ teaspoon salt

1 tablespoon baking powder

200 g caster sugar

40 g unsalted butter, chilled and cut into cubes

225 g smooth mashed potato (1 large cooked potato or 2 small), at room temperature

2 large eggs, beaten

about 150-200 ml whole milk

to finish:

sunflower oil, for deep-frying

2 tablespoons caster sugar

1 teaspoon ground cinnamon

a doughnut cutter, or 7.5-cm round pastry cutter and 1-cm round pastry cutter

a deep-fat fryer or large, deep, heavy-based saucepan

makes 12 doughnuts

Peel, core and chop the apples into small pieces, about the size of your little fingernail. Sprinkle with the cinnamon and toss until thoroughly mixed. Set aside until needed.

Sift the flour, salt, baking powder and sugar into a large bowl. Add the butter and rub it in with the tips of your fingers until the mixture looks like fine crumbs. Work in the mashed potato, then stir in the apple mixture with a round-bladed knife. Add the eggs and enough milk to make a soft but not sticky scone-like dough.

Turn the dough out onto a lightly floured work surface and pat it out to about 1.5 cm thick. Cut into rounds with the doughnut cutter, or use the large pastry cutter and then stamp out the centre rounds with the smaller cutter. Gather up the trimmings and pat them out to make more doughnuts.

Heat the sunflower oil in a deep-fat fryer or large, deep, heavy-based saucepan to 180°C (350°F) or until a cube of bread turns golden in 40 seconds. Deep-fry the doughnuts in batches for 5–6 minutes, turning them frequently, until a good golden brown colour. Remove with a slotted spoon and drain on kitchen paper. Toss in the caster sugar mixed with the cinnamon and leave to cool before eating. These doughnuts are best eaten on the day of making and are not suitable for freezing.

quick cinnamon buns

Warm, sticky, fragrant cinnamon buns are hard to resist but they take hours to make the 'proper' way with a yeast dough. In this shortcut method, the dough is easily mixed in a food processor, then the buns are shaped quickly and baked – all the flavour in less time.

300 g plain white flour

¼ teaspoon bicarbonate of soda

2 teaspoons baking powder

50 g granulated sugar

a good pinch of salt

50 g unsalted butter, chilled and cut into cubes

150 g cottage cheese

3 tablespoons natural yoghurt

about 2 tablespoons whole milk

filling:

4 tablespoons unsalted butter, very soft

50 g light muscovado sugar

1½ teaspoons ground cinnamon

100 g pecan pieces

a brownie tin, 25 x 21.5 cm, well greased

makes 12 buns

Preheat the oven to 200°C (400°F) Gas 6.

To make the dough, put the flour, bicarbonate of soda, baking powder, sugar and salt in the bowl of a food processor. Process just long enough to combine the ingredients. Add the butter to the bowl and process until you have a sandy texture.

Add the cottage cheese, yoghurt and 1 tablespoon of the milk and process until the ingredients come together to make a ball of soft dough. If there are dry crumbs or the dough seems dry and hard, add extra milk, 1 tablespoon at a time.

Turn the dough out onto a lightly floured work surface and roll out to a rectangle about 30 x 23 cm.

Using a round-bladed knife, spread the soft butter evenly over the dough. Mix the brown sugar with the cinnamon and sprinkle over the top, followed by the pecan pieces.

Roll up the dough from one long side to resemble a Swiss roll. Using a sharp knife, cut the roll into 12 even slices. Arrange the buns, cut-side up, in the prepared tin in 4 rows of 3, setting them slightly apart.

Bake in the preheated oven for about 20 minutes, until light golden brown. Set the tin on a wire rack. Leave to cool for 2 minutes, then remove the buns from the tin, gently separate them and eat while still warm.

These buns are best eaten on the day of making and are not suitable for freezing.

apple and sultana scones

Crème fraîche and lemon curd make the perfect additions to these light and fruity scones. The tiny chunks of apple in the dough retain a crisp bite, giving the scones a lovely texture and moistness.

225 g plain white flour

4 teaspoons baking powder

2 tablespoons caster sugar

50 g unsalted butter, chilled and cut into cubes

1 eating apple, peeled, cored and finely diced

40 g sultanas

1 large egg

80 ml whole milk

to serve:

crème fraîche

lemon curd

a biscuit cutter, 5 cm diameter
a baking tray, greased

makes about 12 scones

Preheat the oven to 220°C (425°F) Gas 7.

Put the flour, baking powder and sugar in a food processor and pulse to combine. Add the butter and process for about 20 seconds until the mixture resembles fine breadcrumbs. Transfer to a large bowl, stir in the apple and sultanas, then make a well in the centre of the mixture.

Beat the egg and milk together in a separate bowl, reserving 1 tablespoon of the mixture in another bowl. Pour most of the remaining liquid into the flour mixture and bring together to form a soft dough using a fork. If there are still dry crumbs, add a little more of the liquid. Turn the dough out onto a lightly floured surface and knead briefly until smooth. Gently pat or roll out to a thickness of about 2.5 cm. Cut out rounds with the biscuit cutter, pressing the trimmings together to make more scones.

Arrange the scones on the prepared baking tray, spacing them slightly apart. Brush the tops with the reserved egg and milk mixture and bake in the preheated oven for 10–12 minutes, until risen and golden.

Transfer to a wire rack to cool slightly. These scones are best served split open while still warm and topped with crème fraîche and lemon curd. Once completely cool, store in an airtight container in a cool cupboard and eat within 2 days.

plain scones with strawberry jam and cream

These light and airy scones are closer in texture to cake than bread and have a lovely crumbly texture. They are best served in the traditional way, split open while still warm, topped with strawberry jam and whipped cream and finished off with a fresh strawberry. Simply heavenly!

225 g self-raising flour

1 teaspoon baking powder

2 tablespoons caster sugar

50 g unsalted butter

75 ml whole milk

1 egg

to serve:

strawberry jam

125 ml whipping cream, whipped

small strawberries

icing sugar, to dust

a biscuit cutter, 5 cm diameter
a baking tray, greased

makes about 10–12 scones

Preheat the oven to 220°C (425°F) Gas 7.

Put the flour, baking powder and sugar in a food processor and pulse to combine. Add the butter and process for about 20 seconds, until the mixture resembles fine breadcrumbs. Tip the mixture into a large bowl and make a well in the centre.

Beat together the egg and milk and reserve 1 tablespoon of the mixture. Pour the remaining mixture into the flour and work in using a fork. Turn out on to a floured work surface and knead briefly tomake a soft, smooth dough (work in a little more flour if the mixture is sticky).

Pat out the dough to a thickness of about 2.5 cm and stamp out rounds using a biscuit cutter. Put the rounds on the prepared baking tray, spacing them slightly apart. Brush with the reserved egg and milk mixture and bake in the preheated oven for about 8 minutes, until risen and golden. Transfer to a wire rack and leave to cool slightly.

These scones are best served split open while still warm and topped with strawberry jam, whipped cream and a fresh strawberry. Once completely cool store in an airtight container in a cool cupboard and eat within 2 days.

apple buttermilk scone round

This traditional scone round has a lovely crunchy demerara sugar topping and is packed with juicy apple pieces. Enjoy it warm, spread with butter and lots of apricot preserve, pear and ginger jam or apple marmalade.

*1 large cooking apple or
1–2 crisp tart eating apples
(about 250 g)*

*200 g plain white flour, plus
extra for dusting*

80 g plain wholemeal flour

1 teaspoon bicarbonate of soda

*75 g demerara sugar, plus extra
for sprinkling*

*75 g unsalted butter, chilled
and cut into cubes*

*about 140 ml buttermilk, plus
extra for glazing*

a large baking tray, greased

makes 8 scones

Preheat the oven to 220°C (425°F) Gas 7.

Peel, core and coarsely chop the apple. Mix the flours, bicarbonate of soda and sugar in a food processor. Add the butter and process until the mixture looks like fine crumbs. With the machine running, add the buttermilk through the feed tube to make a soft, but not sticky, dough.

Turn the dough out onto a floured work surface and knead in the apple chunks to form a coarse and lumpy dough. Shape into a ball and put in the middle of the prepared baking tray. With floured fingers, pat the dough into a 22-cm round. Brush lightly with buttermilk to glaze, then sprinkle with a little demerara sugar to give a crunchy surface. Using a sharp knife, score the round into 8 even wedges.

Bake in the preheated oven for about 20–25 minutes, until lightly golden and firm to the touch. Leave to cool on a wire rack. These scones are best eaten warm on the day of making. Once completely cool they can be wrapped then frozen for up to 1 month.

index

conversion charts

Weights and measures have been rounded up or down
slightly to make measuring easier.

Measuring butter:
A US stick of butter weighs 4 oz. which is approximately
115 g or 8 level tablespoons. The recipes in this book require
the following conversions:

American	Metric	Imperial
6 tbsp	85 g	3 oz.
7 tbsp	100 g	3½ oz.
1 stick	115 g	4 oz.

Volume equivalents:

1 teaspoon	5 ml
1 tablespoon	15 ml

American	Metric	Imperial
¼ cup	60 ml	2 fl. oz.
⅓ cup	75 ml	2½ fl. oz.
½ cup	125 ml	4 fl. oz.
⅔ cup	150 ml	5 fl. oz. (¼ pint)
¾ cup	175 ml	6 fl. oz.
1 cup	250 ml	8 fl. oz.

Weight equivalents:		Measurements:	
Imperial	Metric	Inches	cm
1 oz.	30 g	¼ inch	5 mm
2 oz.	55 g	½ inch	1 cm
3 oz.	85 g	1 inch	2.5 cm
3½ oz.	100 g	2 inches	5 cm
4 oz.	115 g	3 inches	7 cm
6 oz.	175 g	4 inches	10 cm
8 oz. (½ lb.)	225 g	5 inches	12 cm
9 oz.	250 g	6 inches	15 cm
10 oz.	280 g	7 inches	18 cm
12 oz.	350 g	8 inches	20 cm
13 oz.	375 g	9 inches	23 cm
14 oz.	400 g	10 inches	25 cm
15 oz.	425 g	11 inches	28 cm
16 oz. (1 lb.)	450 g	12 inches	30 cm

Oven temperatures:

120°C	(250°F)	Gas ½
140°C	(275°F)	Gas 1
150°C	(300°F)	Gas 2
170°C	(325°F)	Gas 3
180°C	(350°F)	Gas 4
190°C	(375°F)	Gas 5
200°C	(400°F)	Gas 6
220°C	(425°F)	Gas 7

recipe credits

LINDA COLLISTER
American biscuits
apple buttermilk scone round
apricot and honey rye bread
banana fudge layer cake
black and white chocolate marble
　loaf cake
blueberry lemon pound cake
breakfast tea loaf
buttermilk cornbread
carrot and almond loaf cake
chocolate crackle cookies
chocolate crumble muffins
chocolate layer cake
cider-apple doughnuts
classic choc chip cookies
classic oat cookies
coconut blondies
cranberry and dark chocolate
　brownies
fresh peach and oat muffins
fresh pineapple layer cake
lemon squares
lemon, almond and blueberry
　muffins
maple pecan loaf
maple syrup pecan cake

Mississippi mud pie
old-fashioned blueberry
　gingerbread
old-fashioned brownies
old-fashioned maple bran muffins
quick cinnamon buns
soured cream and spice brownies
soured cream coffee cake
Thanksgiving cranberry bundt
treacle soda bread
warm chocolate cheesecake

SUSANNAH BLAKE
angel food cake
apple and sultana scones
baby Chelsea buns
coffee and walnut cake
dark chocolate floral cake
gingerbread cupcakes with
　lemon icing
gooey chocolate and hazelnut
　cupcakes
lemon drizzle cake
maple and pecan cupcakes
passion fruit butterfly cakes
plain scones with strawberry jam
　and cream

snow-topped coconut cake
spiced carrot and pistachio cake
sticky coffee bars
strawberry cheesecake cupcakes
toasted teacakes
Victoria sandwich with
　strawberries and cream

MAXINE CLARK
chocolate and banana bread
cranberry and cinnamon
　crunch tart
double chocolate brownie tart
　with walnut crust
double chocolate chip cookies
free-form caramelized peach tart
fresh raspberry tart
little Richmond maids of honour
　tartlets
pumpkin pie
ricotta and muscatel raisin
　cheesecake
simple lemon cheese tart

ROSS DOBSON
carrot and walnut cake with
　cream cheese frosting

classic baked cheesecake
fresh raspberry and almond slices
pear and ginger crumble cake
pear, almond and mascarpone tart
strawberry buttermilk cake
upside-down peach cake

BRIAN GLOVER
key lime pie
lemon and ginger cheesecake
lemon meringue pie
lime and blueberry cake with
　lime syrup

LIZ FRANKLIN
apple loaf cake
white chocolate and raspberry
　tartlets

FRAN WARDE
flapjack squares
pumpkin seed cookies

LAURA WASHBURN
classic apple pie

photography credits

MARTIN BRIGDALE
pages 1, 4 left & right, 6, 31, 38,
　40, 41, 42, 45, 46, 49, 57, 58,
　62, 69, 70, 72, 75, 76, 79, 85,
　100, 112, 120, 121, 122, 125,
　126, 129, 132, 133, 137, 138,
　145, 146, 148, 154, 156, 161,
　162, 168, 171

RICHARD JUNG
pages 3, 4 centre, 5, 10, 13, 22–23,
　24, 25, 26, 28–29, 81, 84, 90,
　94, 97, 98, 116, 119, 131, 142

KATE WHITAKER
pages 2, 35, 54, 82, 107, 130, 141,
　151, 152, 164, 167

PHILIP WEBB
pages 50, 53, 80, 93, 103, 104, 155,
　158, 172, 173

DIANA MILLER
pages 17, 18, 20, 21, 61, 65, 66,
　86, 89

PETER CASSIDY
pages 47, 108, 115, 165, 170, 176

DEBI TRELOAR
pages 30, 92, 102, 150

LISA LINDER
pages 110, 111, 134

CAROLINE ARBER
pages 14, 37

JONATHAN GREGSON
pages 96, 136

TARA FISHER
pages 56, 64

WILLIAM LINGWOOD
pages 36, 88

PATRICE DE VILLIERS
pages 51, 52

JEAN CAZALS
page 128

WILLIAM REAVELL
pages 32

CHRIS TUBBS
page 74

POLLY WREFORD
page 16